Accession no.
36230371

D0476774

Studying for your
Nursing
Degree

**CRITICAL
STUDY SKILLS**

Critical Study Skills for Nursing Students

Our new series of study skills texts for nursing and other health professional students has four key titles to help you succeed at your degree:

Studying for your Nursing Degree

Academic Writing and Referencing for your Nursing Degree

Critical Thinking Skills for your Nursing Degree

Communication Skills for your Nursing Degree

Register with **Critical Publishing** to:

- be the first to know about forthcoming nursing titles;
- find out more about our new series;
- sign up for our regular newsletter for special offers, discount codes and more.

Visit our website at: 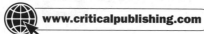 **www.criticalpublishing.com**

Our titles are also available in a range of electronic formats. To order please go to our website www.criticalpublishing.com or contact our distributor NBN International by telephoning 01752 202301 or emailing orders@nbninternational.com.

CRITICAL
PUBLISHING

Studying for your
Nursing
Degree

LIS - LIBRARY

Date	Fund
29/5/18	nm-WAR
Order No.	
2875767	

University of Chester

**CRITICAL
STUDY SKILLS**

JANE BOTTOMLEY AND STEVEN PRYJMACHUK

First published in 2017 by Critical Publishing Ltd
Reprinted in 2017

All rights reserved. No part of this publication may be reproduced, stored in a retrieval
system, or transmitted in any form or by any means, electronic, mechanical, photocopying,
recording or otherwise, without prior permission in writing from the publisher.

The authors have made every effort to ensure the accuracy of information contained in this publication,
but assume no responsibility for any errors, inaccuracies, inconsistencies and omissions. Likewise every
effort has been made to contact copyright holders. If any copyright material has been reproduced
unwittingly and without permission the Publisher will gladly receive information enabling them to
rectify any error or omission in subsequent editions.

Copyright © (2017) Jane Bottomley and Steven Pryjmachuk

British Library Cataloguing in Publication Data
A CIP record for this book is available from the British Library

ISBN: 978-1-911106-91-3

This book is also available in the following e-book formats:

MOBI: 978-1-911106-92-0
EPUB: 978-1-911106-93-7
Adobe e-book reader: 978-1-911106-94-4

The rights of Jane Bottomley and Steven Pryjmachuk to be identified as the Authors of this work
have been asserted by them in accordance with the Copyright, Design and Patents Act 1988.

Text and cover design by Out of House Limited
Project management by Out of House Publishing
Printed and bound in Great Britain by Bell and Bain Ltd, Glasgow

Critical Publishing
3 Connaught Road
St Albans
AL3 5RX
www.criticalpublishing.com

MIX
Paper from
responsible sources
FSC® C007785

Contents

Acknowledgements

We would like to thank the many university and nursing students who have inspired us to write these books. Thanks are also due to Anita Gill, John Morley, Rob Marks, and Sasiporn Ounjaichon.

Jane Bottomley and Steven Pryjmachuk

Meet the authors

Jane Bottomley

is a Senior Language Tutor at the University of Manchester and a Senior Fellow of the British Association of Lecturers in English for Academic Purposes (BALEAP). She has helped students from a wide range of disciplines to improve their academic skills and achieve their study goals. She has previously published on scientific writing.

Steven Pryjmachuk

is Professor of Mental Health Nursing Education in the School of Health Science's Division of Nursing, Midwifery and Social Work at the University of Manchester and a Senior Fellow of the Higher Education Academy. His teaching, clinical and research work has centred largely on supporting and facilitating individuals – be they students, patients or colleagues – to develop, learn or care independently.

Introduction

Studying for your Nursing Degree is the first book in the *Critical Study Skills for Nurses* series. The *Critical Study Skills for Nurses* series supports student nurses, midwives and health professionals as they embark on their undergraduate degree programme. It is aimed at all student nurses, including those who have come to university straight from A levels, and those who have travelled a different route, perhaps returning to education after working or raising a family. The books will be of use both to students from the UK, and international students who are preparing to study in a new culture – and perhaps in a second language. The books also include guidance for students with specific learning difficulties.

Studying for your Nursing Degree introduces you to university life and helps you to understand what you need to know and do to meet the requirements of your degree programme. It guides you through the systems and procedures which you will encounter, at the same time 'demystifying' some aspects of academic culture. It will help you acquire, develop and put into practice the knowledge, skills and strategies you need to succeed at university and in your professional practice. Throughout the book, there is an emphasis on particular aspects of learning which are highly valued in academic life and in the nursing professions: **learner autonomy**, **critical thinking** and **reflective practice**.

Between them, the authors have many years' experience of both nursing practice and education, and academic study skills. All the information, text extracts and activities in the book have a clear nursing focus and are often directly linked to the **Nursing and Midwifery Council's Code**. There is also reference to relevant institutional bodies, books and journals throughout.

The many activities in the book include **reflections**, **case studies**, **top tips** and **tasks**. There are also advanced skills sections, which highlight particular knowledge and skills that you will need towards the end of your degree programme – or perhaps if you go on to postgraduate study. The activities often require you to work things out and discover things for yourself, a learning technique which is commonly used in universities. For many activities, there is no right or wrong answer – they might simply require you to reflect on your experience or situations you are likely to encounter at university; for tasks which require a particular response, there is an answer key at the back of the book.

These special features throughout the book are clearly signalled by icons to help you recognise them:

  Learning outcomes;

  Quick quiz or example exam questions/assessment tasks;

  Reflection (a reflective task or activity);

 Task (usually a more practical or written task);

  Case studies;

  Top tips;

  Checklist;

  Advanced skills information;

  Answer provided at the back of the book.

Students with limited experience of academic life in the UK will find it helpful to work through the book systematically; more experienced students may wish to 'dip in and out' of the book. Whichever approach you adopt, handy **cross references** signalled in the margins will help you quickly find the information that you need to focus on or revisit.

We hope that this book will help you to develop as an aware, independent, critical and reflective learner and practitioner, and that it will guide you towards success in your chosen study path at university.

A note on terminology

In the context of this book, the term 'nursing' should be taken to include 'nursing, midwifery and the allied health professions', wherever this is not explicitly stated. There is an **Appendix** on the **language of higher education** at the back of the book which you can consult as you work through the text.

Chapter 1
Studying nursing in higher education

Learning outcomes

After reading this chapter you will:

- have gained knowledge of higher education and its place in the UK education system;
- understand some of the terminology and 'jargon' used in higher education;
- have gained knowledge of institutions which set standards for nursing education;
- have gained knowledge of levels and qualifications in nursing;
- understand the relevance and importance of lifelong learning and continuing professional development;
- understand the importance of student autonomy and independent learning in universities;
- have gained knowledge of how courses are structured and delivered.

This chapter will develop your knowledge and understanding of the study of nursing in UK universities. It will outline the 'qualification frameworks' that are relevant to becoming, and developing as, a nurse, and discuss the role of important educational and professional bodies. In addition, you will be introduced to the types of teaching and learning that you will encounter as a student nurse.

Before you read the chapter, test your knowledge with the Quick quiz below. You can revisit the quiz as you read, or come back to it after reading the whole chapter to see if your answers have changed. Key words in this chapter are highlighted in **bold** and can be found in the glossary in the Appendix.

CROSS REFERENCE

Appendix, The language of higher education

Quick quiz

1) What does HE stand for?
2) How is HE different from FE?
3) What are the main qualifications offered by universities?
4) Which is the higher level qualification, a *degree* or a *diploma*?
5) What is the minimum academic qualification you need to become a registered nurse?
6) What mark (percentage) do you usually need to obtain a *first-class* degree?
7) What are 'credits' and how can you get them?
8) What do you think 'Accreditation of Prior Learning' might be?
9) What is 'lifelong learning'?
10) What are the most common types of assessment in universities?

What is HE?

HE stands for **'higher education'**, one of two options in UK **tertiary education**, ie education available to people of 16 years or above.

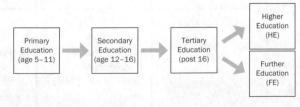

Figure 1.1: The UK education system

HE is mainly provided by universities, and principally awards **degrees** and **diplomas**. In contrast, **further education** (**FE**) is provided by colleges, which deliver courses and award qualifications which are **vocational** in nature (NVQs; City & Guilds; BTEC), preparing people directly for the workplace. However, in recent years, there has been a blurring of the line between the two types of institution, with many FE colleges, sometimes in association with partner universities, also offering degrees. This is one way of making degrees accessible to a wider range of people, some of whom may find it convenient to attend classes in a local FE college or to study in the evenings. Recently introduced 'degree apprenticeships', which offer the potential to obtain a degree while learning on the job, also blur the boundaries between vocational and academic learning.

Your nursing degree

Nursing and midwifery in the UK are today fully integrated into the HE sector. Although there is a large vocational component to these subjects, based on practical and clinical skills, they also require highly developed intellectual skills, and universities are considered to be the best place for students to acquire and develop these. Nursing is thus an academic subject, equivalent to any other, such as medicine, engineering or English literature, and therefore measured against the same standards.

Qualification frameworks

HE qualifications, sometimes called 'academic awards', are regulated across the UK via two frameworks: the Quality Assurance Agency for Higher Education in England, Wales and Northern Ireland (QAA, 2008), and the Quality Assurance Agency for Higher Education in Scotland (QAA, 2014). These frameworks help institutions and employers judge the value of an individual's education and help ensure equity between academic subjects. Table 1.1 shows the academic levels assigned by the QAA to each stage of HE, and provides information on how they relate to a study pathway in nursing.

Table 1.1: An overview of academic levels in relation to nursing study in HE

UNDERGRADUATE STUDY			
England, Wales, Northern Ireland	**Scotland**	**Award**	**Notes**
Level 4	Level 7	Certificate of Higher Education (CertHE)	
Level 5	Level 8	Diploma of Higher Education (DipHE) Foundation Degree (FdD)	Up until 2010, minimum academic qualification for nurses
Level 6	Level 9	Ordinary Bachelor's Degree eg BSc Nursing	Minimum academic qualification for nurses and midwives; common exit point in Scotland
	Level 10	Bachelor's Degree with Honours eg BSc (Hons) in Nursing Studies, BNurs (Hons), BMidwif (Hons)	Usual academic qualification for nurses and midwives in England, Wales and Northern Ireland

Table 1.1: (*cont.*)

POSTGRADUATE STUDY			
Level 7	Level 11	Master's Degree eg MSc, MA, MPhil Postgraduate Certificate or Diploma (PGCert; PGDip)	Minimum academic qualification for Advanced Practitioners
Level 8	Level 12	Research Doctorate (PhD) Professional Doctorate eg DNurs, MD, ClinPsychD	Recommended qualification for Advanced Practitioners who are Nurse Consultants

An undergraduate degree has four classifications. These are shown in Table 1.2, along with the marks usually required at each level.

Table 1.2: Bachelor's degree classifications and typical required marks

CROSS REFERENCE

Chapter 6, Assessment

CLASSIFICATION	MARKS REQUIRED
1st	Above 70%
2:1	60–69%
2:2	50–59%
3rd	40–49%
Fail	Below 40%

Courses and credits

You can see from Table 1.1 that, in order to enter the nursing profession, you must obtain a degree from an HE institution, usually a university. If you study full time, it will take three years to obtain an honours degree (or four years in Scotland). However, universities recognise that this timescale is not possible or ideal for many people, so they have flexible learning systems which allow students to fit study into their lives in a practical way.
This can involve:

- **distance learning**, where the student mainly studies from home via correspondence, using web-based resources – perhaps occasionally attending university workshops etc;
- **blended learning**, which combines traditional classroom study and web-based learning;
- **part-time study** (including the new degree apprenticeships mentioned earlier).

Flexible learning is facilitated by the **credit** points system which underpins HE education. Each course **module** that you study has a number of credit points attached to it. Each credit is equal to 10 hours of study, either in class, or through self-study (QAA, 2008, 2014). These credit points build up to eventually form your degree, whether over three years' full-time study, or over a longer period if you study part time. Table 1.3 shows that a student has to earn 360 credit points in order to be awarded an honours degree.

Table 1.3: HE qualifications in relation to credit points

ACADEMIC QUALIFICATION	CREDIT POINTS REQUIRED
CertHE	120 at Level 4 (Scotland Level 7)
DipHE	120 at Level 4 (Scotland Level 7) + 120 at Level 5 (Scotland Level 8)
Degree with Honours (Ordinary Degree in Scotland)	120 at Level 4 (Scotland Level 7) + 120 at Level 5 (Scotland Level 8) + 120 at Level 6 (Scotland Level 9)

Look at the QAA frameworks (2008, 2014) online to see descriptors detailing exactly what is expected of a student at each level. Note that not all universities offer the CertHE. Some universities in England, Wales and Northern Ireland may offer an ordinary degree without honours to students who have obtained a certain number of credits at Level 6. A four-year Scottish Honours Degree requires an additional 120 credits at Level 9/10.

Universities provide students with information on each module with regard to its academic level and the number of credit points it carries. Many modules, often called 'core modules', will be obligatory; some modules will be optional. All modules are organised around the following:

- a set of **learning outcomes** which identify what you will be able to do or understand by the end of the course;
- a process of **teaching and learning** which will help you achieve the learning outcomes;
- **assessment** which will measure your achievement and provide evidence of it.

Top tips

Thinking about 'the big picture'

Learning outcomes, teaching and learning, and assessment will be aligned, so you should think about 'the big picture' and consider them together. When preparing for assessments, for example, look again at the learning outcomes to check what you will be expected to demonstrate. In class, think about how the classroom activities are partly preparing you for assessment, and ask if you are not sure.

CROSS REFERENCE

Chapter 3, Becoming a member of your academic and professional community, Reflective practice

Accreditation of Prior Learning (APL)

Credit points can sometimes be assigned for prior learning or experience, through a process known as Accreditation of Prior Learning (APL). There are two branches of APL:

1) Accreditation of Prior Certificated Learning (APCL) allows you to transfer any credit points you already hold from one institution to another. One example of this is when English registered nurses holding only a diploma (having qualified before 2010) decide to 'top up' to an honours degree by completing 120 credit points at Level 6.

2) Accreditation of Prior Experiential Learning (APEL) allows you to acquire credit points for your practical or professional experience, provided that it meets the academic standards demanded by the university involved. To support an application for APEL, a university will often require a **portfolio** of evidence, ie a reflective account (usually written) of your learning experiences.

CROSS REFERENCE

Chapter 6, Assessment, Portfolios

While this transfer system allows for flexibility in HE, note that it can often be a very complicated process, with institutions sometimes disagreeing on the transfer values of particular modules.

Reflection

- List examples of your own practical or professional experience which you think would be valid in terms of APEL, along with examples of evidence you could provide as support. (An example is provided.)

EXPERIENCE	SUPPORT
managed a team of nursing assistants	written reflection outlining the management skills I demonstrated; feedback from colleagues, including those who I managed; analysis of the strengths and areas for development in my management style

Lifelong learning and continuous professional development

The flexible approach to study outlined above is underpinned by the much-valued educational principle of **lifelong learning**. Lifelong learning, by definition, extends beyond your degree, and may involve postgraduate study or general professional development. If you are a registered nurse with a degree or diploma, lifelong learning may involve taking post-registration modules, sometimes called 'standalone modules', which are offered by many universities. These could help you top up a diploma to an honours degree, or, if you already have a degree, they could help you generally in your **continuing professional development (CPD)**.

CPD in nursing is regulated by the Nursing and Midwifery Council (NMC). This body specifies the amount of professional training and updating that should be undertaken by practising nurses and midwives via a process known as 'revalidation'. Currently, this is prescribed as 35 hours of CPD in a three-year period, at least 20 hours of which must be 'participatory learning', that is, learning activity involving interaction with other health professionals.

Case study

- How is CPD demonstrated in the personal account below?

"I am a nurse and a member of the military, and I've been a nursing lecturer for 20 years. I think moving between a clinical setting and a classroom setting was very good for developing my professional skills. During that time, I applied skills from the clinical setting to the classroom setting, and in the classroom, I was able to develop some skills around confidence and critical thinking to apply in a clinical setting. In order to advance in the military, I also had to do training, particularly related to good discipline. Now I am pursuing my PhD in nursing, so that means I will develop as a scholar. During the process of studying for my PhD, I feel like I can develop my professional skills and become a complete nursing scholar when I go back home to Thailand. I need to learn more and search for new knowledge in order to be innovative in nursing. No one is too old to learn. Actually, my mom is a nurse, and now she's 70 years old, and she likes to learn new things about nursing using her smartphone and the internet. She's particularly interested about care for the elderly because she herself is trying to find ways to be independent in later life."

Senior military nurse and University of Manchester PhD student

Reflection

What do you think your priorities in terms of CPD will be when you qualify as a registered nurse?

Being a university student

Reflection

- What is your previous experience of study? Which of the following have you experienced? Was your experience positive or negative? Why was this?
  1) Big classes where the teacher talks a lot and the class mostly listens
  2) Large lectures with hundreds of students
  3) Small seminar groups where people discuss topics or articles
  4) One-to-one tutorials with a teacher

University culture and practices may not always reflect your past educational experiences. Some students may find it difficult to work things out at first.

Case studies

- Do you think these students have a good understanding of what is expected of them at university level? What advice would you give them?
  1) "My course looks quite easy – there aren't many lectures and I don't have to hand in any essays until the end of the semester. So it looks like I'll have a lot of free time!"
  2) "The lecturer puts some things on Blackboard after the lecture, but I'm not very confident with technical stuff so I haven't seen it."
  3) "It doesn't matter if I miss lectures – I can get all the information I need from reading textbooks."
  4) "I'm very nervous about speaking in front of people so I tend to keep my head down in seminars and just get through them without drawing attention to myself."
  5) "I'm disappointed in my essay mark and don't understand what I did wrong – I worked really hard on it! But there's nothing I can do about it now. Maybe I'm just not cut out for this."

The students quoted above have some common misunderstandings about university life. These areas of confusion are dealt with in the following sections, to demonstrate, among other things, how study is not just about the time you spend in the classroom, why it is important to go to lectures, when and how you should seek support from academic staff, and why, sometimes, you might just need to push yourself beyond your comfort zone in order to achieve your full potential!

Study time

CROSS REFERENCE

Chapter 2, Strategies for effective learning

At university, you will encounter a range of teaching and learning methods, including those which involve face-to-face contact with academic staff, ie **lectures**, **seminars** and **tutorials**. However, you may find that there seems to be a lot of 'free' time on your timetable. Hence, it is important to understand that the time you spend with your lecturers is only a small part of your study. A 10-credit module is seen to represent approximately 100 hours of actual work (QAA, 2008, 2014). So if you attend, say, 30 hours of lectures on a particular 10-credit module, this still leaves 70 study hours of study to complete outside the classroom. This may involve searching the library, reading, planning and writing essays, improving your computer skills, or collaborating with other students on a group project.

Top tips

Getting the most from your study time

Try thinking of your full-time studies as a typical 'working week' of about 35–40 hours a week, 7–8 hours a day, and plan your time accordingly. (Adapt this if you are studying part time.) Take sensible breaks throughout the day, just as you would if you were working – maybe cook a nice healthy lunch to give you energy, or take the dog for a walk to give your brain some much-needed downtime!

Virtual Learning Environments

Study outside the classroom is often facilitated by Virtual Learning Environments (VLEs) such as **Blackboard** or **Moodle**. VLEs contain vital information on the course and links to useful resources. They also host a number of useful tools. For example, VLE discussion boards can enable interaction with your peers and with the lecturers. VLEs are also important in terms of assessment: you may be required to complete some assessment tasks online, and you will probably be required to upload written assignments onto your VLE using plagiarism-detection software such as **Turnitin**, which compares your writing with published sources and other submitted essays to ensure it is all your own work. You may also receive assessment feedback online.

Top tips

Getting the most from your VLE

1) Check your VLE frequently as there may be new announcements or documents. Staff will just assume that you will look at these; they will not chase you up to make sure you've accessed them. It is your responsibility to be on top of things.

2) Spend some time learning how to navigate the site so that you can access things quickly when you need them. The more you use the site, the easier this will get.

3) Read your discussion board contributions carefully before clicking 'send'. Make sure that the style is appropriately polite and that there is no ambiguity – especially if it could cause offence. Also check your grammar and punctuation – poor writing can detract from the seriousness of your message.

4) Check if it's possible to download slides before lectures – this could help you to be more prepared for lectures, and facilitate the note-taking process.

Lectures

Lectures at university are designed to provide an overview of a topic. As such, they are a very useful starting point. They are also a springboard for further reading, thinking, discussion and writing. The aim of lectures is not just to reproduce what is in the books: the lecturer can guide you towards the most important aspects of a topic, or provide you with a theoretical framework on which to 'hang' the ideas you accumulate from your reading. They may direct you towards particular chapters in textbooks or indicate how different journal articles relate to the topic, as well as each other. Lectures can also be enjoyable! A lecturer may present you with interesting examples, or offer up lively anecdotes which can bring a subject to life. Some lecturers may include interactive activities, for example, getting you to use mobile phone apps or 'clickers' (a device used to provide on-the-spot analysis of students' responses during a lecture), or they may encourage comments and questions.

Top tips

Getting the most from lectures

1) Experiment with different note-taking strategies: linear notes, mind maps, diagrams etc.

2) Use headings and sub-headings to organise your notes, or use colour to highlight thematic patterns.

3) Experiment with taking hand-written notes and using your laptop or tablet to see which suits you best.

 4) Put together a list of useful abbreviations and get into the habit of using them. Some common ones are listed below. Match them to the full term (as with the example that has been given) to check your understanding:

eg   that is to say
NB   compare and contrast
cf   for example
ie   note

5) If you find it difficult to keep up in lectures, ask if the lecturer is willing to upload the lecture slides onto the VLE beforehand, so that you can do some preparation and maybe check out some difficult terminology beforehand. If the slides are available, you could upload them onto your laptop or tablet and annotate them as you follow the lecture.

6) Go over your notes as soon as possible after the lecture, when it is fresh in your mind. Improve the organisation if you can, adding or refining headings, sub-headings and cross references – this is easier of course with typed notes.

7) Find a lecture 'buddy' who you can discuss the lecture with afterwards. You could check if you agree on what the main points are, or try to clarify anything you were confused about.

8) Look back at previous lecture notes before attending the next one.

Seminars

On some courses, small seminar groups will provide an opportunity for you to follow up on the lecture, to clarify points and expand your understanding. You may be asked to read an article beforehand, and one or two students may be asked to lead the seminar by presenting their summary and opinion of the article, before a general group discussion.

It can be difficult to contribute in seminars: for some people it is rather nerve-wracking; many find it hard to interject – particularly if there are some dominant personalities (maybe yours!) in the room. But remember you are all in the same boat – you all have your strengths and weaknesses, you all have something to learn – and the lecturer is there to bring out the best in you, not put you on the spot!

Top tips

Getting the most from seminars

1) Be prepared. Think about two or three points you would like to make, and think about how you might express them.

2) Say something early on in the seminar if you can. Once you take the plunge and contribute, the second time will be much easier.

3) Use seminars as an opportunity to 'talk through' and test ideas that you are exploring. This can often be a good way of preparing for an essay.

4) Don't be afraid to ask for clarification – if you haven't understood something, then there is a good chance that others haven't either!

5) Be prepared to provide clarification yourself. It is often necessary to reconsider the way we express ourselves in order to achieve clarity; this reformulation process is also a way of helping us to understand if we have truly grasped an idea.

6) Listening is just as important as speaking. Be prepared to learn from others – and to challenge them (politely) when you disagree.

7) There is a certain etiquette to be followed in seminars. It is expected that people will disagree with each other on some points, but this is usually done in a very careful way, often using 'balanced' expressions such as:

"I see what you mean, but …"

"I take your point, but …"

"I agree to some extent, but …"

Some 'negative' questions (considered less direct than normal questions) are also useful, eg:

"Wouldn't you say that …?"

"Don't you think that …?"

"Isn't it the case that …?"

"Aren't we forgetting the impact of …?"

CROSS REFERENCE

Communication Skills, Chapter 2, Participating in seminars and meetings

Tutorials

Some universities and courses will offer one-to-one tutorials with a lecturer, often to discuss general progress, give feedback, or help you prepare for an essay or dissertation. Most academic staff will also have **office hours**, when you can visit them in their office and raise any queries. If you are worried about your progress or your marks, it is important that you use this opportunity to seek advice.

Top tips

Getting the most from tutorials

1) Be prepared. The lecturer's time is probably very limited, so spend some time thinking about how you can make the best use of a meeting by preparing some focused questions.

2) Questions which are 'closed', ie questions which simply require a *yes*/*no* answer, are quicker and easier to deal with than questions which are 'open'. Compare:

"How should I obtain my data?" (open question)

"Would a questionnaire be a good way of collecting data in this case?" (closed question)

The first question puts the onus on the lecturer and requires them to do all the thinking. The second question shows you have thought about things and are now merely making good use of the expertise of the lecturer. The second question is not only easier and quicker to deal with, it also shows that you are taking responsibility for your learning, which will probably lead to a better relationship with the lecturer.

3) If you are not sure you've understood something, briefly summarise the message you think you are receiving from the lecturer to double check.

CROSS REFERENCE

Chapter 2, Strategies for effective learning, Managing your learning: student autonomy

CROSS REFERENCE

Communication Skills, Chapter 3, Getting the most from tutorials

Independent learning

Studying as an adult at university may be very different to what you experienced at school. At school, for many reasons, there may have been a lot of direct instruction from the teachers, where they talk and you listen. At university, there is more emphasis on guiding you towards working and thinking independently, with the lecturer acting as a facilitator, adviser or resource: this is known as **independent learning**, something which is highly valued in universities.

As a university student, you are expected to take responsibility for, and manage, your own learning at all times. This involves recognising what you need to do to study successfully, and finding out how to do it. Independent learning requires self-motivation, self-direction and self-discipline. The lecturers will guide you; they will offer support and encouragement. But they

CROSS
REFERENCE

Chapter 2,
Strategies
for effective
learning,
Managing
your learning:
student
autonomy

will not hold your hand; they will not do your work for you or solve your problems. This is not because they are lazy or don't care what their students do; it is because they believe in the educational principle of **student autonomy**, whereby a student takes charge of their own learning. They are convinced that encouraging you to take responsibility for your learning will make you a better student, a better thinker and, ultimately, a better nurse: it will, among other things, prepare you for the requirement to '*be accountable for your decisions*' in professional practice (NMC, 2015, p 10).

A commitment to independent learning is part of a kind of contract between you and the university. This contract also covers the things you can in turn expect from the university.

Top tips

Knowing your rights and responsibilities

Make sure you look at your university's 'Student Charter', sometimes called an 'Educational Contract', a document which tells you what you should expect from the university, and details your own responsibilities as a student.

CROSS
REFERENCE

Chapter 4,
Critical
thinking

One teaching and learning method commonly adopted by university lecturers to encourage independent learning is **directed study**. This is where the lecturer sets a task and offers some guidance; but it is your responsibility to complete the task, even if you are not required to formally submit it: some tasks are assessed, but others may simply have the aim of contributing to your long-term development. Directed study may involve **problem-based learning**, where you find solutions to real-world problems. This is often achieved by means of **collaborative learning**, ie working collectively and co-operatively with other students. The lecturer may or may not be present; they may or may not intervene. You, the students, are in control of the learning process. During these tasks, you will develop skills which are essential for nursing practice, in which you are required to '*work co-operatively*' and to '*share your skills, knowledge and experience for the benefit of people receiving care and your colleagues*' (NMC, 2015, p 8).

CROSS
REFERENCE

Chapter 2,
Strategies
for effective
learning,
Collaborative
learning

One of the main aims of activities such as problem-based learning is to help you develop your **critical thinking** skills, your ability to analyse and evaluate information and ideas. Great emphasis is placed on critical thinking in education and in nursing practice.

In the university learning environment, there may be a certain amount of role reversal in class, whereby a student takes on a typical teacher role. This could include giving a presentation or leading a seminar. Many students can feel very nervous about this kind of activity, but remember that there are techniques you can adopt to help you perform better.

For information on how you are assessed at university, see Chapter 6.

Summary

CROSS
REFERENCE

Chapter 6,
Assessment

This chapter has examined the place of nursing in the UK HE system, and the role of key institutions that set standards for nursing education, such as the QAA and the NMC. It has discussed the practicalities of nursing study in terms of the qualifications and degree classes that can be awarded, as well as the credits system that underpins university courses. It has explored the notion of lifelong learning, and it has looked closely at current modes of teaching and learning, with a particular emphasis on independent learning and student autonomy. With this knowledge and understanding, you will be well-equipped to begin your journey as a student nurse.

References

NMC (Nursing and Midwifery Council) (2015) *The Code: Professional Standards of Practice and Behaviour for Nurses and Midwives* [online]. Available at: www.nmc.org.uk/globalassets/sitedocuments/nmc-publications/nmc-code.pdf (accessed 16 March 2017).

QAA (Quality Assurance Agency for Higher Education) (2008) *The Framework for Higher Education Qualifications in England, Wales and Northern Ireland* [online]. Available at: www.qaa.ac.uk/en/Publications/Documents/Framework-Higher-Education-Qualifications-08.pdf (accessed 16 March 2017).

QAA (Quality Assurance Agency for Higher Education) (2014) *The Framework for Higher Education Institutions in Scotland* [online]. Available at: www.qaa.ac.uk/en/Publications/Documents/FQHEIS-June-2014.pdf (accessed 16 March 2017).

Chapter 2
Strategies for effective learning

Learning outcomes

After reading this chapter you will:

- have improved your understanding of the learning process;
- have developed strategies for managing your university studies effectively;
- have learned about different theories of learning and understand what kind of learning styles can be effective for you;
- be able to adapt to situations that require you to work independently or collaboratively.

This chapter will explore ideas around learning and enable you to identify which learning strategies could help you meet the expectations of university study. Adopting the right approach to your studies will maximise your potential and enable you to reach your goals.

What is learning?

When you learn, it may be for 'learning's sake', ie to satisfy your curiosity, to improve your mind and to grow as an individual. Or you may learn for a defined purpose or goal. Being a university student ideally involves both these aspects of learning.

Learning is not a question of pouring information and ideas into an empty student vessel! Nor is it something which will just happen as a matter of course if you simply turn up to class. Some learning may be more or less 'unconscious', ie when you just 'pick things up' without really realising it at the time. But most learning, particularly in an academic context, is an active process which requires specific intellectual skills.

Learning is not just a question of finding and remembering facts. It involves many stages and processes as you encounter and explore new information and ideas. Figure 2.1 gives some examples (adapted from Devine, 1987: xix).

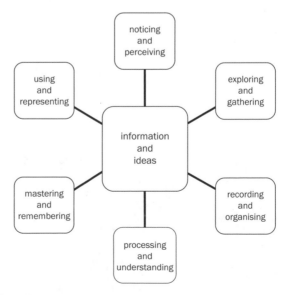

Figure 2.1: The learning process

Something like 'noticing' may seem like a very basic human activity, but noticing key facts, patterns and relationships is actually an essential part of being an intelligent, critical learner, and, importantly, it is something that you can get better at. As you explore, gather, record, and organise facts and ideas, you are employing your analytical and evaluative skills to reveal and understand how things relate and compare. This is how you begin to process and assimilate information and ideas. This processing continues as you work to make sense of all you have learned. When you use and represent the knowledge and understanding you have acquired, in an essay for example, you demonstrate your understanding of the subject, proving that learning has actually occurred!

As you study at university, there are three questions which you need to ask:

- *What* do I need to learn?
- *Why* do I need to learn it?
- *How* should I learn it?

This chapter will help you work out *how* you can learn most effectively. If you can find ways of learning which suit your personality and circumstances, draw on the qualities and skills you already possess to some degree, and encourage personal and intellectual development, you are much more likely to enjoy and benefit from the learning process.

Managing your learning: student autonomy

Universities have identified a set of 'graduate attributes' that students should develop as they pursue their studies (discussed in more detail in Chapter 3).

One key graduate attribute is '*personal and intellectual autonomy*' (Jenkins, 2009). Being autonomous means managing your own learning, and taking responsibility for it. This means you should be able to recognise and address your own learning needs, and to work out – through experimentation – which learning styles or strategies will serve you best. You need to develop an awareness of which qualities and skills facilitate learning, and consider how you can personally improve in these areas. All of this is underpinned by one particular quality: the capacity for **reflection**, ie standing back from a situation or experience in order to critically analyse and evaluate it so that you can understand and learn from it. This is something which is also central in a nurse's **reflective practice**, '*a process by which you can think about and achieve a better knowledge and understanding of your practice, learning from your own experiences in order to improve the care you provide to patients*' (Lee-Woolf et al, 2015, p 12).

Autonomy is not always easy to achieve, but it should ultimately make you more effective in your studies and in your professional life. It could also make you happier! Surveys often reveal a strong correlation between autonomy and job satisfaction (see for example, Marks, 2014), including among nurses (Zangaro and Soeken, 2007).

The qualities and skills which can facilitate autonomous learning, such as being reflective, organised or proactive, you no doubt already demonstrate to a greater or lesser extent in your everyday life. University is a chance to develop them still further, with a view to applying them across your studies and in your future professional life. This is why universities use the terms 'graduate attributes' or 'transferrable skills', which explicitly link your development at university with your overall personal development and future endeavours.

CROSS REFERENCE

Chapter 3, Becoming a member of your academic and professional community, Graduate attributes

CROSS REFERENCE

Chapter 3, Becoming a member of your academic and professional community, Reflective practice

Reflection

1) Consider some of the main qualities and skills associated with student autonomy and successful learning:

good organisation, discipline, being realistic, resilience, being positive, being pro-active, commitment, motivation, being determined, flexibility, adaptability, innovation, initiative, being open-minded, intellectual curiosity, creativity, reflection, self-awareness

2) Think of situations where you have demonstrated some of these in your everyday life, and areas of your current studies where you might apply them successfully. (Some examples have been given.)

QUALITY/ATTITUDE	EVERYDAY LIFE	CURRENT STUDIES
Being well organised	eg managing my children's after-school activities	eg could organise my lecture notes better using file dividers
Being disciplined	eg writing a shopping list before going to the supermarket – and sticking to it!	eg should put my phone on silent and out of reach while studying
Being resilient (eg recovering from setbacks, persevering, keeping a sense of perspective)	eg took my driving test three times and eventually passed	eg should try to talk to lecturers about negative feedback on an essay to see how I can improve next time – instead of burying my head in the sand!

Strategies for effective learning

You will have opportunities to develop the qualities and skills in the reflection above throughout your studies at university. This section provides you with some general advice to get you started in the right direction.

Being organised

1) Use simple organisational tools to plan your time, activities and environment. These could include:

- weekly timetables – universities often put individual weekly timetables online via the student portal;
- academic diaries (from September to June), to record classes, events, exams, deadlines etc;
- electronic calendars like Microsoft Outlook – your university will probably provide training for these;
- notebooks or smart phones – jot down or store to-do items as they come to you and transfer them to a more permanent format later if necessary.

2) Include independent study periods on your timetable, with details on what, where and how you plan to study.

3) Remember to factor in the rest of your life! Many students have to juggle study with work, bringing up a family, or an important interest, hobby or commitment. Include these things in your calendars, timetables or diaries.

4) Organise your work space at home. Make it clear to others that this is where you work and that it is important to you.

5) Plan ahead. Plan to get your assignment finished well before the deadline. This will leave you enough time to read through and make minor alterations or corrections. It also means that you will not get stressed by last-minute issues with computers or printers.

Being disciplined

1) Prioritise the tasks on your to-do list, allot a reasonable amount of time to each one, and stick to this.

2) Identify times when you could feasibly study, and make sure that study time is really study time. Use any formally scheduled independent study or reading time to do just that – study and read!

3) Don't allow study to spill over too much into non-study time. Maintain clear boundaries, otherwise you may become over-tired and demotivated.

4) Make a start. Beware of 'displacement activities', chores around the home that suddenly seem more urgent when you are due to start that essay! Make yourself do at least 30 minutes study before doing anything else. By that time, you may have found a 'way into' your essay and the work may seem less daunting; if you are still 'stuck', then leaving it alone for a while and occupying yourself with something else (like the ironing!) may be the sensible option.

5) Take regular breaks. Your brain will get tired, and work may well look different when you look at it with fresh eyes.

Being realistic

1) Do not use studying as an excuse to banish friends, exercise, reading or housework from your life. It is not practical or effective to spend all your time studying, and you will probably lose concentration and get distracted anyway. Also, if you lose control of important aspects of your life, such as keeping on top of your finances, you will only end up worrying when you should be studying or sleeping. It is important to achieve a work–life balance.

2) Remember that your studies also include clinical practice, and it is likely that your academic year will be longer and more demanding than that of students studying other disciplines. This means that, while it is important that you experience normal student life, you may have to moderate your activities. For example, it is clearly not a good idea to go to a student party the night before you are on clinical placement.

Being smart

1) Multitask by, for example, reading or listening to an educational podcast on the bus.

2) Develop efficient note-taking strategies when reading or in lectures. Think about using a laptop or tablet.

3) If you have module options, make sure you choose the right ones. It is important to choose things that you are most interested in, if you can, but it is also important to consider which options will help you achieve your short- and long-term goals. For example, you may choose an option related to where you want to work when qualified.

4) Learn what is valued in your discipline, and what will get you good marks. For example, as mentioned earlier in this chapter, **reflective practice** is critical to nursing and it is unlikely that you will get good marks in the later years of your programme if you haven't grasped this concept.

5) Always seek out and follow guidelines and protocols in clinical practice. And while you are expected to think critically and challenge guidelines and protocols where there is a lack of evidence to support them, make sure you do this tactfully, by discussing things calmly with your mentor, for example; otherwise, it could be seen as sabotage.

6) Make yourself aware of individual staff preferences. There may be general departmental guidelines on formatting, for instance, but you may find that some lecturers prefer you to use 1.5 spacing, whereas others prefer double spacing. (Others may not have a preference, as long as

you are clear and consistent.) Remember that you want to make the *actual* reader's experience as smooth and enjoyable as possible, so it is worth spending time considering how you can do this.

Being positive

1) Embrace positive thinking. Being a student is going to be a big part of your life for a long time, so it is important that studying doesn't become some terrible chore that you constantly dread. You will be a better student if you can find as much as possible of the learning process interesting and enjoyable. Some of it may even be fun!

2) You will make many lifelong friends on your course, friends you will able to turn to and share with when things get tough. They will no doubt have had similar experiences.

Being proactive

1) If you don't know something, think about how you can find it out; if you don't know how to do something, think about how you might work it out. You will find a lot of helpful information in course handbooks and on VLEs. You will be expected to read the relevant documentation regarding the aims, learning outcomes, content and assessments relating to each of your courses, and to seek guidance if there is something that you don't understand.

2) See the big picture. Try not to look at tasks in isolation: find out how they fit into the course overall. Consider not only why you are being asked to do something, but why you are being asked to do something at a particular time or in a particular way. For example, a course on 'research methods' may seem quite abstract to you at the beginning of your studies, but if you look at the information provided in the course handbook on the research dissertation you will be required to carry out in the future, it will make more sense to you.

3) Some people find it easier to manage their studies if they arrange to work with others. If you are alone, it can be very easy to find those 'displacement activities': that pile of ironing can suddenly seem quite tempting compared to a pile of heavy reading! But if you've committed to a study meeting with others, you probably won't want to let them down. Just remember that studying together must not lead to collusion: you can learn together, but, unless it is a group assignment, that learning must then be directed into an individual assessment which is entirely your own work.

4) If you have, or think you may have, a specific learning difficulty, seek support. Universities have special departments which are likely to be able to provide services to meet your needs.

5) Note that being 'supernumerary' in nursing practice, ie additional to the required clinical workforce, does not mean you cannot or should not take part in nursing activities. Use every opportunity to learn and demonstrate your abilities, whatever stage you are at in your nursing course.

Being committed

1) Commit yourself to your studies. It can be tempting to believe that getting things out of the way with as little effort as possible will bring satisfaction, but often, students report that the most satisfying tasks are those they put the most effort into. Looking at an essay that you've rushed off at the last minute can be a very dispiriting experience. It's something you've probably detached from because you just want it out of the way. On the other hand, printing out an essay that has been carefully considered and crafted, up to and including precise formatting, will usually bring you a great deal of satisfaction. And, whatever mark you receive, if it's for an essay you care about, it will mean more to you. If it's a good mark, you will feel proud and motivated to continue in the same vein; if it's a disappointing mark, you will care more about obtaining feedback, and the criticisms will probably relate more to concrete things you can change. If you receive a poor mark for a slap-dash essay, you already know why you've done badly!

2) Commitment means doing everything you can to manage your own circumstances at any given time. This includes contacting your tutors and lecturers when you have academic and/or personal issues, rather than burying your head in the sand or plodding on heroically. They are very experienced in student matters and you probably won't be telling them anything they haven't heard before.

Being open-minded

1) Be aware of the benefits that could come through working with others. Be alert to what you can learn from those around you, including other students.

2) Healthcare is constantly changing, so you need to get used to change. Try to approach change as an opportunity rather than an irritation – unless you have real professional concerns about it, in which case raise them with a mentor or manager.

3) Accept that you will, like everyone – experience uncertainty at times, and that it is no shame to admit this – it is all part of the learning process.

Being reflective and self-aware

1) Everyone makes mistakes. The important thing is to learn from them. It is also important to be conscious of and confident about what you do well. After all, if you are not aware of your own strengths and limitations, how will you be able to help colleagues and patients work on theirs?

2) Think about how you can use feedback from lecturers and your peers to improve your performance.

3) Learn to look at your own work with a critical eye. Try reading an essay out loud to see if it makes sense, for example.

4) Compile a reflective journal to record your responses to your student and clinical experiences.

5) Understand your own learning preferences, and the alternatives available to you, and be prepared to experiment. This will be discussed in the next section.

Learning styles

A learning style is a particular way of acquiring, processing and using information or ideas. At this stage in your life, you will have developed certain approaches to learning new things. The premise in this chapter is that there is no right or wrong way to study, but that it is beneficial for students to explore options and to experiment. In this section, you are encouraged to reflect on your experience and to consider some theories of learning. This process may confirm your intuitions about what is best for you, or it might persuade you to investigate alternative approaches to learning.

Reflection

1) Think of things you have learned to do in the past (eg learning to drive or swim, learning a language or a new technology, learning karate or Zumba).
2) Which were positive learning experiences?
3) Which were negative learning experiences?
4) What is it that made them successful or not?
5) Which of these things were within or outside of your control?

While reflecting on your past learning experiences, you may have identified certain common threads in your approach to learning, and these may be reflected in the many theories of learning which exist. These theories are of interest to students because they can suggest useful learning strategies. However, there is disagreement about their validity, and so they should be viewed with a critical eye.

Some theories of learning suggest that your learning behaviour and preferences are connected to your personality. One of the most well known (though not universally accepted – see Willingham et al, 2015) of these suggests that different people learn better through different senses.

- **Visual** learners are said to learn better when they can see things. This may involve reading or watching videos. They are advised to use colour coding and pictures in their notes.

- **Aural/Auditory** learners are said to learn better when they can hear things and speak to people. This may involve reading the essays they've written out loud. They are advised to meet regularly with other students to talk through prescribed reading or assessment tasks, and to use podcasts.

- **Kinaesthetic** learners are said to learn better when they can touch things or bring out the physical side of something. This may involve creating posters or investigating issues through role play. They are advised to organise information onto interactive physical charts or picture boards.

This sensory model is sometimes referred to as the VAK model (Dunn et al, 1984), later expanded to the VARK model, which includes **Reading and Writing** preferences (Fleming and Mills, 1992). Alternative theories of learning divide people along other lines, according to whether they are, for example, introvert or extrovert, visual or verbal, intuitive or analytical. Honey and Mumford (1982) divide people into four learning types: activists, reflectors, theorists or pragmatists. They suggest that most people are likely to stick to one or two of these, depending on their personality. However, they also propose that some of these styles are better suited to particular types of *activity*, concluding, therefore, that it is important for everyone to develop a range of approaches.

Being aware of these different learning models and the ideas behind them offers you an opportunity to think how you might personalise your learning. However, as mentioned above, some scholars question the evidence base of these theories of learning (see for example, Willingham et al, 2015), so it is important to assess them critically. Keep an open mind, but do not label yourself or restrict the options available to you. And remember the importance of the learning context, the conditions under which you learn, or the nature of the task or activity with which you are faced. What's more, be aware that things don't always go to plan, as demonstrated in the case studies below.

Case studies

- Consider the following situations. What advice would you give?

  1) Lectures send Sarah to sleep! The problem, however, is that lectures are an important part of the course and attendance is monitored. What is the solution?

  2) Craig feels more engaged with his studies when he works with others. He meets a great group of like-minded people on his course. He invites them round to his halls, and together they produce an impressive piece of work for the next assignment. What problems might Craig and his friends encounter?

  3) Wen Li is a night owl! She works best at night: this is when her mind really gets going, and she can often work productively until the early hours of the morning. However, she is scheduled to do a week of early starts (7am) in clinical practice. How will she be able to maintain her previously successful strategy?

  4) Eva is a single parent. She has family help with childcare in the day time but in the evening, with the TV on all the time, and phones constantly on the go, she finds it hard to find the quiet space with no distractions that suits her. What can she do?

Discussion of case studies

There are no simple answers to the problems described in the case studies above, but it is worth considering the following if you find yourself in a similar situation:

1) Sometimes it is necessary to do things you don't enjoy. Question whether there is something you can do to change the situation: sit at the front instead of the back; change your note-taking method. If all else fails, investigate 'lecture capture' options.

2) This could work well with a group assignment, but if it is an individual assignment, be careful that collaboration does not turn into collusion. Also, although group work can be a very positive experience, there are often problems with sharing out workload and acknowledging everyone's contribution fairly. Furthermore, be aware that it's not always possible to work with people you know and get on with. The reality at university and in the workplace is that you may have to work with anyone, and that you may have to negotiate difficult relationships. Indeed, negotiating relationships is an essential part of nursing.

3) It depends. Can you survive on four hours of sleep? Former UK Prime Minister Margaret Thatcher famously claimed to! But most people cannot. Also, it's worth asking if your mind really does work better at that time or if you've persuaded yourself of this because you like to lie in!

4) There are no easy solutions when it comes to juggling work and family life. You could try to arrange extra childcare to allow you to study in the library for an hour or so before you go home. If this is not a practical option for you, you could attempt to get the TV and phones turned off for a set time (not an easy task!) while the kids do their homework and you study. Another alternative could be to wait until the kids go to bed before you study, but this could affect your alertness the next day.

In the end, the right learning approach for you in a particular situation is whatever gets the best results! The important thing is to be aware of what facilitates learning and what hinders learning for *you*, generally or in a particular situation. Be prepared to abandon unsuccessful study strategies and try out new ones, even if it means venturing out of your comfort zone. Experimentation and trial and error are part of learning and part of life, and these involve taking risks, making mistakes, reflecting on experience, and seeking and accepting feedback and advice. One of the joys of developing as a student or professional is 'the light-bulb moment', where you realise where you are going wrong or what really works for you.

Case studies

- Look at the comments below. Could you benefit from any of the strategies these people adopted? Have you had any similar 'light-bulb moments' about your own work and study habits?

1) "I used to get the bus to work, and tried to do some reading for my part-time Master's en route. But it was often hard to concentrate – the bus was crowded and noisy and I worried about missing my stop. Then, to save a bit of money, I started to walk to work – it takes about 30 minutes. I instantly felt better knowing I was doing some exercise and getting some fresh air every day, especially as I was spending so much of my day hunched over a computer. But I became aware of another unexpected advantage. I found that when my brain was free to 'wander', I often started to think about what I'd written the night before, and I was suddenly seeing what I'd written on the page in a different way. Stepping away from the page allowed me to make sense of things, to see how everything hung together, to see new patterns and relationships. I then couldn't wait to get back to the writing and rejig it. Certainly more productive than reading the same paragraph three times on the bus!"

2) "On my computer, I would write a little bit towards my essay, get some ideas down, make some notes for finishing off later. When I was really motivated, I would work for hours uninterrupted but there often came a point when I just stared at the screen and nothing seemed to happen. I could not get my words to make sense. What I learned was that if I left my work at this point (perhaps it was my brain telling me to stop) – for a couple of hours, a day or maybe a week, but not too long – things made much more sense when I went back to them."

Top tips

Mindmaps and MindGenius

If you feel that diagrammatic representations facilitate your learning (ie that you are a 'visual' learner, according to the VAK model (Dunn et al, 1984)), you could find that **mind maps** are useful. Mind maps are an image-centred system for recording and categorising information. If you find mind maps are your thing, you may wish to investigate **MindGenius**, a tool for 'computer-aided thinking'. It allows you to create mind maps on screen in an editable format. It may be particularly useful for students with learning difficulties such as dyslexia. Interfacing with Microsoft Word and PowerPoint means that it can be used to create essays and presentations.

Collaborative learning

The importance and necessity of independent learning has been explained in this chapter. However, universities also value another type of learning very highly: **collaborative learning**. Collaborative learning is an approach to learning that involves '*joint intellectual effort by students, or students and teachers together*' (Smith and MacGregor, 1992, p 1).

There are many ways in which you could be asked to work with your peers at university, including:

- group projects;
- group presentations;

- seminars;
- clinical placements;
- simulated learning, for example, in clinical skill labs or via role play;
- peer marking, eg marking the work of your fellow students as a way of exploring task requirements.

Libraries and learning commons often have group study facilities to accommodate this important aspect of learning at university.

Reflection

1) Think of some of the advantages that could come from working collaboratively with others.

2) Think of some occasions when you have been part of a group.

3) Was it a positive or negative experience? Below are some suggested positive outcomes of group work and collaboration. Did you experience any of these?

- having a sense of being part of a learning community;
- feeling supported;
- achieving more than you might be able to alone;
- hearing diverse and stimulating perspectives and experiences;
- learning different ways to do things;
- clarifying your own ideas through discussion;
- learning to make a point effectively;
- acquiring interpersonal skills;
- having the opportunity to take on different roles;
- acquiring leadership skills;
- gaining confidence;
- learning to deal with being challenged and criticised;
- socialising;
- preparing for the practices of the workplace.

Collaboration in nursing

The type of interpersonal skills that come into play when you work collaboratively are highly valued not just by universities, but by employers. In professions like nursing, collaborative working is essential to deliver the standards expected by the public. Indeed, collaborative working is an essential part of the Nursing and Midwifery Council Code (NMC, 2015), eg:

2.1 work in partnership with people to make sure you deliver care effectively

3.3 act in partnership with those receiving care, helping them to access relevant health and social care, information and support when they need it

In fact, Section 8 of the Code, fully reproduced below, is based on co-operation:

8 Work co-operatively

To achieve this, you must:

8.1 respect the skills, expertise and contributions of your colleagues, referring matters to them when appropriate

8.2 maintain effective communication with colleagues

8.3 keep colleagues informed when you are sharing the care of individuals with other healthcare professionals and staff

0.4 work with colleagues to evaluate the quality of your work and that of the team

8.5 work with colleagues to preserve the safety of those receiving care

8.6 share information to identify and reduce risk

8.7 be supportive of colleagues who are encountering health or performance problems. However, this support must never compromise or be at the expense of patient or public safety.

Collaboration in action

Independent learning and collaborative learning are by no means mutually exclusive. Students working together in groups or teams will most often be working autonomously from the lecturers, while at the same time drawing on their collective knowledge and resources to complete a task, solve a problem etc. Furthermore, group work will often involve both group and individual elements. Figure 2.2 represents the possible dynamics of a group presentation, where the group has responsibility for the ideas, and how they are organised and represented visually (eg through PowerPoint), and the individual has the responsibility both to contribute to group work and to deliver part of the presentation directly to an audience. It is important to understand this dynamic. If for example, you just focus on getting your own bit right, your mark could still be affected by weaknesses in the general organisation of ideas. Similarly, it is mainly the group, not the individual, who will usually be given credit for the brilliant idea you focus on in your own part. The group can also provide constructive input on each other's individual performance during presentation practice. Sometimes the marking system will include separate marks for the group and the individual (though these are often hard to separate completely – a good idea is better if it is conveyed to the audience in an engaging way by an individual presenter, and a group presentation will be more successful if its constituent parts are as good as they can be).

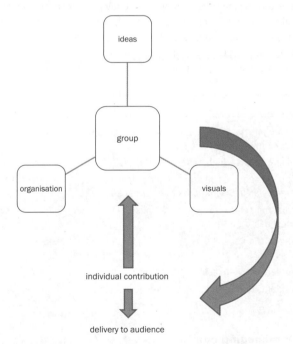

Figure 2.2: Group presentations

Other group tasks will work in a different way. In a group writing project, for example, you will have to work together to:

- identify and distribute reading/research tasks fairly and efficiently;
- find productive ways of sharing information and using it to devise a structure and framework for the written report;
- decide if you will have individuals writing different parts of the report, or if you will try some collaborative writing activities;

- determine how the whole thing comes together;
- format and proofread the report – discovering who in the group has these important skills is a key task.

Important qualities in group work

Participants in group work require certain qualities and skills, eg:

- being a good listener;
- being ready to learn from others;
- being confident about what you have to offer;
- getting your message across;
- giving and receiving constructive criticism;
- giving and accepting support from others;
- being aware of group dynamics so that you can help the group 'gel' and avoid serious problems;
- identifying the roles that you and others can play to be effective group members and so get the most out of all members of the group;
- putting the needs of the group before your own while also using the experience for personal development;
- being self-aware and reflective so that you can improve your collaborative skills.

Managing conflict

Group work, by its very nature, often provokes conflict. While it is probably safe to say that a degree of conflict is a normal part of group work, it is of course necessary to manage it in some way. In the early part of your studies, lecturers may provide support to facilitate the way you work together, but as you progress, this type of facilitation will probably decrease or disappear. You will be relied upon to find your own solutions to challenges that arise.

Reflection

1) What kind of conflicts do you think may arise in group work? Have you experienced any of these things? How did you respond?
2) Here are some issues which commonly arise. How might you manage or resolve these issues?
   - some students not 'pulling their weight', leaving others to feel the mark awarded to the group is affected by an individual's poor performance;
   - some students not taking the task seriously – not turning up for meetings or shirking their responsibilities;
   - some students dominating, not allowing participation from the whole group – especially quieter students – resulting in some students feeling left out;
   - some students relying on lecturers to resolve conflict;
   - some students forming cliques or even bullying other students.

Discussion: managing conflict

There is no one answer to any of these problems, but the following may help.

What the group can do:

- create and maintain channels of communication (meetings, email, Facebook, WhatsApp);
- set some 'ground rules' (communication, attendance, punctuality, turn-taking, phone etiquette, role allocation etc);
- include everyone in the group and be careful not to discriminate for any reason;
- find a way of negotiating with each other in a calm, sensitive and respectful way;

- be clear about the purpose of each meeting and the tasks you are involved with – think about using an agenda;
- in meetings, arrange the physical environment so that everyone can see and hear everyone else;
- manage negativity – encourage the discussion of solutions rather than just focusing on problems;
- spend some time investigating each other's strengths (PowerPoint, proofreading, communication within the group, understanding statistics etc), so that the workload can be more effectively distributed – rotate roles if this seems fairer;
- keep a record of what decisions are taken and who is responsible for what;
- create a relaxed atmosphere in meetings – a plate of biscuits might help!

What you can do:

- remember that if the group succeeds, so do you, so it is worth taking a positive approach;
- be prepared for meetings; do what you have been asked to do; if you weren't able to do something, apologise and explain;
- be kind, helpful and encouraging to others, especially if they are struggling. This is a good thing to do *per se*, but remember that people also learn a lot by explaining things to others;
- adopt positive body language when others are talking – make eye contact, smile etc;
- respond to others with affirmation, comments, questions etc when appropriate;
- when you speak, acknowledge and build on what others have said where appropriate;
- be gentle and constructive in your criticisms – avoid nastiness and blaming people;
- if you don't understand, ask – it is likely that others are in the same boat;
- you may wish to look at some of the information provided by ACAS (the Advisory, Conciliation and Arbitration Service; see, for example ACAS, 2014), an independent body whose remit is to improve relations between employers and employees.

CROSS
REFERENCE

*Communi-
cation Skills,*
Chapter 2,
Participating
in seminars
and meetings

Summary

This chapter has explored some of the strategies available to you as you strive to become an effective learner, meet the expectations of university study and achieve your own personal goals. It has discussed various approaches to learning, with the aim of encouraging you to identify and explore approaches which might work well for you, without limiting your options. Finally, it has examined the role of collaborative learning in HE.

References

ACAS (2014) *Managing Conflict at Work* [online]. Available at: www.acas.org.uk/media/pdf/h/r/Managing-conflict-at-work-advisory-booklet.pdf (accessed 16 March 2017).

Devine, T (1987) *Teaching Study Skills*. Newton, MA: Allyn and Bacon.

Dunn, R, Dunn, K and Price, G (1984) *Learning Style Inventory*. Lawrence, KS: Price Systems.

Fleming, N and Mills, C (1992) Not another Inventory, Rather a Catalyst for Action. *To Improve the Academy*, paper 246 [online]. Available at: http://digitalcommons.unl.edu/podimproveacad/246/ (accessed 16 March 2017).

Honey, P and Mumford, A (1982) *Manual of Learning Styles*. London: P. Honey.

Jenkins, A (2009) *Research-Teaching Linkages: Enhancing Graduate Attributes* [online]. Available at: www.enhancementthemes.ac.uk/docs/publications/research-teaching-linkages-enhancing-graduate-attributes-overview.pdf?sfvrsn=20 (accessed 11 January 2017).

Lee-Woolf, E, Jones, J, Brooks, J and Timpson, J (2015) Essentials of Nursing: Values, Knowledge, Skills and Practice. In Burns, D (ed) *Foundations of Adult Nursing*. London: Sage.

Marks, N (2014) Guardian Readers Reveal What Makes Them Happy at Work. *The Guardian* [online]. Available at: www.theguardian.com/sustainable-business/happy-work-what-makes-you (accessed 16 March 2017).

NMC (Nursing and Midwifery Council) (2015) *The Code: Professional Standards of Practice and Behaviour for Nurses and Midwives* [online]. Available at: www.nmc.org.uk/globalassets/sitedocuments/nmc-publications/nmc-code.pdf (accessed 16 March 2017).

Smith, B and Macgregor, J (1992) What is Collaborative Learning? In Goodsell, A, Maher, M, Tinto, V, Smith, B and MacGregor, J (eds) *Collaborative Learning: A Source Book for Higher Education*. University Park, PA: National Centre on Postsecondary Teaching, Learning and Assessment, Pennsylvania State University.

Willingham, D, Hughes, E and Dobolyi, D (2015) The Scientific Status of Learning Style Theories. *Teaching of Psychology*, 42(3): 266–71.

Zangaro, G and Soeken, K (2007) A Meta-Analysis of Studies of Nurses' Job Satisfaction. *Research in Nursing and Health*, 30: 445–58.

Chapter 3
Becoming a member of your academic and professional community

Learning outcomes

After reading this chapter you will:

- have gained an understanding of the values and principles which underpin your discipline and the wider HE community;
- have gained an understanding of some of the practices and conventions of your discipline and the wider HE community;
- have developed your understanding of how knowledge is developed in HE;
- have begun to gain an understanding of how knowledge and language relate to each other;
- have gained an understanding of the concept of 'graduate attributes'.

A university can be seen as an 'academic community', a group of academic practitioners (people who teach, learn and do research) who share a particular way of thinking about the world. This chapter explores the challenges that you might face as you strive to become a member of this community and enter the specific disciplines of nursing and midwifery. This chapter also introduces the concept of 'graduate attributes' and discusses their relevance to your studies.

Joining the academy

It is notable that Becher (1989), in a landmark study of universities and those who cultivate knowledge across the many existing disciplines, refers to the different groups found in universities as 'tribes', with their own cultures, or 'territories'. Becoming a student means joining one of these 'tribes' and functioning within its 'territory'. This can be a real challenge. As with all social interactions, there are certain codes of behaviour, or 'rules', that need to be followed. What's more, although some of these codes or rules may be explicit, others can appear to be rather hidden or obscure: rules regarding the payment of fees, or the return of library books are usually clearly signalled and easy to understand, but 'rules' on how to address your lecturers or even how to reference academic sources can be harder to decipher – and are often understood through trial and error. Moreover, these are things which often vary across disciplines and institutions, and even according to individual preferences.

Case studies

- Think about the situations below. What do you think would be the best way to proceed in each case?

1) You are going to meet your academic adviser for the first time. You've heard that people use first names rather than surnames and titles in British universities, but this is very different from your country and you don't really feel comfortable with it.

2) You need to email a lecturer for the first time and you are not sure of the most appropriate way of wording or structuring it.

3) You have been instructed to write 'formally' in your essays but you thought you were already doing this!

4) You have been told that your work is not 'critical' but do not really understand what this means.

5) You have been informed that 'plagiarism' is a very serious issue and it has made you feel very nervous about using too much information from books and articles.

CROSS
REFERENCE

*Communi-
cation Skills*

Discussion of case studies

1) It is true that it is common to address lecturers, and even professors, by their first names in universities in the UK. This can seem rather strange, especially for students who come from cultures where a more formal acknowledgement of status and hierarchy is expected. What's more, it can cause confusion, because the use of first names can imply the absence of a hierarchy, and this is not really the case: while there is usually a fairly relaxed, collaborative relationship between students and academic staff in UK universities, this does not mean that anything goes! It might be a good idea in this case to start by using the lecturer's title (Dr Gonzalez, Professor Mason); they may well ask you to call them by their first name from that point on.

2) Use a fairly standard, semi-formal email such as the ones below. It is common in this type of email communication to use certain fixed phrases which can be reused on other occasions; the emails below contain some of these phrases.

> Dear Dr Snow,
>
> I would like to meet with you briefly to discuss my clinical placement. Could you please let me know when your office hours are?
>
> Thank you in advance for your assistance.
>
> Best wishes,
> Karin

> Dear Professor Suliman,
>
> Please find attached my report on dementia care.
>
> Many thanks for your advice on this assessment.
>
> Regards,
> Maria

CROSS
REFERENCE

*Academic
Writing and
Referencing*,
Chapter 4,
Language in
use, style

Over time, the emails may become less formal ('Hi' instead of 'Dear'; first names instead of surnames; 'Best' instead of 'Best wishes'), but you should maintain a formal tone if you are at all unsure.

CROSS
REFERENCE

*Academic
Writing and
Referencing*,
Appendix
1, English
language
references

3) You could perhaps arrange to meet with the lecturer who gave you the feedback to find out what it is exactly that is too informal. Are you using conversational words such as 'actually'? Are you using personal language like 'I really think' or 'you should realise'? Is the text too 'chatty' and lacking in structure? You could also consult a textbook on academic writing (eg Baily, 2014; Bottomley, 2014; Swales and Feak, 2012), or find out about the resources in your university. Most universities have library resources with information on academic writing, and most have in-sessional writing classes where you can receive expert guidance. You may be able to book a 'writing tutorial', sometimes called a 'writing consultation', which will provide you with personalised help, either using a piece of writing you are currently working on, or one that has been returned to you with a mark and comments from a lecturer. In the latter case, the writing tutor will be able to help you understand why you received the mark and feedback you did. Also, remember that good dictionaries label informal and slang words, so always check if you are at all unsure; if you've never used a word before, you should always check it in the dictionary and look at typical examples of the word in use.

CROSS
REFERENCE

Chapter 4,
Critical
thinking

4) Criticality is a difficult abstract concept. Being critical involves analysing, interpreting and evaluating information and ideas. It requires an active reading of the literature to discern relationships and patterns. It necessitates using ideas and evidence from the literature to support and develop your own argument. Some students may have academic skills relating to criticality when they start university but many do not; universities usually understand this and often work with first-year students to help them develop the critical reading and writing skills they need in subsequent years.

5) Plagiarism is indeed a serious issue, but it is one which is often misunderstood. It is certainly not the same thing as making a lot of references to sources, which is actually a very good thing! Problems can arise for international students because of differences between how different academic cultures

treat sources. Issues also sometimes surface if students do not have the confidence to allow their own voice to come to the fore in an essay. Again, it might be a good idea to seek out writing support from the library or in-sessional writing classes and tutorials. Also, many universities offer VLE courses on 'academic malpractice' which will help you to understand what the issues are and how to avoid plagiarism and other forms of malpractice.

Top tips

Being informed

Universities generally have an obligation to say what they expect from you, and what you can expect from them in return. Indeed, you might find these expectations enshrined in a formal document such as an 'Educational Contract' or 'Student Charter', or they might be embedded in a course handbook. These documents (or links to them) are usually given to students in the first week or so of starting university. As an adult learner, it is up to you to read these documents. If you are unsure of anything, it is also up to you to ask questions.

Academic principles, pursuits and practices

Joining the academic community will be easier if you are fully aware of why universities exist and what it is that the people in them believe.

Teaching, research and knowledge

The two pillars of university life are **research** and **teaching**. Universities have strong beliefs about how research should be conducted and how **teaching and learning** should occur. This affects, among other things, how students are expected to engage in learning and how they will be assessed.

Universities are committed to the pursuit and advancement of **knowledge**. This knowledge is presented, discussed and tested through specific '*communicative events*' with a particular shared purpose. These academic '*genres*' (Swales, 1990, p 58) include lectures, research papers, essays and exams, each characterised by particular content and conventions.

As a university student, it is not enough to simply acquire and demonstrate knowledge; university study requires the acquisition of a set of intellectual skills that become increasingly complex as you move through your academic career. In your first year, the emphasis will largely be on achieving and demonstrating **understanding** of concepts and theories in your field; in subsequent years, this understanding will be need to be underpinned by **criticality**; postgraduate (Master's or Doctoral) level studies will almost certainly expect you to perform an **intellectual synthesis** of theories and concepts relevant to your field (pulling these theories and concepts together to create a broad understanding and generate new theories and concepts).

In order to be able to engage with knowledge in your field in a meaningful way, it is important that you understand what knowledge is and how it typically advances in academia.

Task

- Look at the following real-life examples from medicine. What do they tell you about knowledge?

What causes stomach ulcers?

Up until the late 1980s, the prevailing view was that stomach ulcers were caused by stress and lifestyle – a fairly common view still among lay people. In the 1980s, however, Robin Warren and Barry Marshall, two doctors from Australia, put forward the idea that stomach ulcers were caused by the *Helicobacter pylori* bacteria, a claim met with scepticism and even derision, in particular from the manufacturers of the market-leading stomach ulcer medications. Warren and Marshall nevertheless persevered, and, through dogged

CROSS
REFERENCE

Critical Thinking Skills

CROSS
REFERENCE

Academic Writing and Referencing, Chapter 3, Referring to sources

CROSS
REFERENCE

Chapter 4, Critical thinking

CROSS
REFERENCE

Academic Writing and Referencing, Chapter 2, Referring to sources

determination and the assiduous collection of scientific evidence, they managed to persuade the medical community to accept their view. This culminated in their being awarded a Nobel prize in 2005.

Does HIV cause AIDS?

The bulk of the scientific community believes that HIV does in fact cause AIDS. However, there are some who question this view, notably Professor Peter Duesberg at University of California. Only time will tell if Duesberg and others are misguided, or if, conversely, they have in fact been able to see things in the data that others could not.

The examples above should help you recognise that much remains unknown in academia, and that knowledge is usually advanced in small steps, often with many wrong turns along the way. For this reason, there is a certain tolerance of uncertainty and ambiguity, and an acceptance of the idea that the more you learn, the less straightforward things tend to become. Scholarship is advanced in part by researchers approaching the literature critically, and thus identifying and exploring **'gaps'** or problems in the current knowledge. The research they do can be **quantitative** (research including 'quantities', ie numbers) or **qualitative** (researched concerned with 'qualities', ie experiences, feelings, perceptions etc). In nursing and a number of other disciplines, **mixed methods** research – research that combines quantitative and qualitative research – is becoming more common. Research findings are usually presented (or 'disseminated') in research reports in academic journals, and you will be required to read these as part of your studies.

Advanced skills

CROSS
REFERENCE

*Academic
Writing and
Referencing*

Research reports

A postgraduate nursing dissertation or thesis, and sometimes an undergraduate research dissertation, may be a report on a piece of research you have carried out. Research dissertations in nursing usually follow an **IMRAD** structure, the most prominent organisational structure used in scientific journals.

This approach to writing about research can be summarised in simple terms as follows:

- **I**ntroduction – what was your research and why did you do it?
- **M**ethod – how did you do it?
- **R**esults – what did you find out?
- **D**iscussion – what does it all mean?

An **I**ntroduction highlights a 'gap' or a problem that your research will address, together with its context and background. It tells the reader why the research is important, and prepares the ground for your study by presenting a **literature review**, that is to say, a critical analysis and evaluation of the current scholarship on the topic, out of which your own argument has emerged. The way you write your introduction is very important, as this is your opportunity to grab the attention of your reader and persuade them of the importance and the logic of your argument.

A **M**ethodology details the way you go about collecting and analysing your data. Your method should be presented in such a way that it can be easily replicated by others. Scholars (or assessors) will scrutinise this to help them judge the validity of your findings.

A research dissertation must include a summary and analysis of the **R**esults. **Figures** and **Tables** may be particularly useful tools in this section.

A research dissertation ends with a **D**iscussion of the meaning, significance and implications of your findings. This section will almost certainly contain a discussion of the limitations of the study, and possibly recommendations for further study.

There may also be a **Conclusion**, which usually outlines the implications for practice in nursing and midwifery. A research report also includes an **Abstract** at the beginning which summarises the study and the main findings. The report concludes with a list of **References** and any **Appendices**.

Values, beliefs and academic integrity

Every community has its own culture, and universities are no different. Academic culture is characterised by particular **values** and **beliefs**. Universities value, among other things, **independent thinking**, **intellectual curiosity** and **freedom of speech**. They believe in **evidence-based** enquiry and activity. They maintain that systems and processes should be **rigorous** and **transparent**. They promote **objectivity** and **criticality**. Of course, all of these are ideals, and like all ideals, they are not always achieved – but they are aspired to. All members of the academic community, including you, play a part in meeting these aspirations.

Academic integrity refers to the moral principles aspired to by universities. One way that universities seek to promote academic integrity is through the use of **reputable sources** and accurate attribution through **referencing**; they consequently see **plagiarism** as one of the most serious attacks on their culture and values.

Another important aspect of academic integrity is **ethical awareness**. This means behaving according to a strict moral code. The implications of this with regard to nursing are discussed later in this chapter, when the Nursing and Midwifery Code is discussed.

CROSS REFERENCE

Academic Writing and Referencing, Chapter 3, Referring to sources

Communication

Academics and students are expected to communicate their knowledge and ideas in a clear, professional way, following the conventions of their discipline. This is particularly the case in those disciplines – including nursing – that involve significant interaction with the public.

Academic phrasebank

Like any community, the academic community has a shared language. While specialist knowledge and terminology varies across disciplines, there are certain things that all members of the academic community do (as discussed in the last section), and they all make use of certain set phrases and structures to do it. At the University of Manchester, a 'bank' of such phrases and structures has been developed through the analysis of academic texts. These are categorised according to functions, ie the things academics *do* with language. Some common categories (related to the ideas discussed in this chapter) and phrases/structures are explored in the task below. Note the *non-committal* tone of many of the phrases, which reflects the many *uncertainties* surrounding knowledge in academia.

CROSS REFERENCE

Academic Writing and Referencing, Chapter 3, Coherence in texts and arguments

CROSS REFERENCE

Academic Writing and Referencing, Chapter 4, Language in use, Clarity

Task

Match each of the functions (numbered) below with a set of phrases and structures (identified by letters A, B, C, etc).

Functions:

1) Identifying knowledge gaps
2) Putting forward an argument
3) Providing evidence
4) Making reference to sources
5) Evaluating sources
6) Acknowledging uncertainty, contradiction and ambiguity
7) Explaining implications

Phrases and structures:

A _____

In his seminal text, Potter explored the social implications of …

The pioneering work of Gonzalez remains crucial to our understanding of …

The article provides a valuable insight into …

The main weaknesses of the study lie in its failure to …

B _____

There has been a great deal of research into this area.

Previous studies have established that …

Suvaris argues that …

While acknowledging the need for further research into this area, McVey concludes that …

C _____

The data supports this.

The evidence to date suggests that …

This can be seen most obviously in the case of …

In a recent study, it was found that …

D _____

To date, there has been little research into the issue of …

The effects of this remain unclear.

What is not yet clear is …

Little attention has been paid to …

E _____

Taken as a whole, these results suggest …

These findings suggest a role for …

This study strengthens the case for …

The implications of these findings are clear.

F _____

However, taking into consideration the small sample size, …

Correlation, of course, does not equal causality.

The data must be interpreted with caution, as …

It is important to allow for bias in the responses due to …

See the website for more examples: www.phrasebank.manchester.ac.uk/

The nursing community

Nursing practice is underpinned by essential knowledge and values, developed over time, and represented in recent years in the Nursing and Midwifery Code.

Historical landmarks in nursing

As in any discipline, knowledge and values have emerged out of particular landmarks in the history of nursing, some of which are briefly outlined below.

Table 3.1: Landmarks in the history of nursing (Isaac, 2015; Lee-Woolf et al, 2015; Pryjmachuk, 2011)

Nineteenth and early twentieth century	Gradual professionalisation of nurses, with the First World War raising the profile of nursing and providing impetus for formal registration
1916	Establishment of the College of Nursing (today the **Royal College of Nursing**), which worked to further raise the profile of nursing and establish a formal nursing register (although nursing was not officially recognised as a profession for almost a hundred years)

Table 3.1: (*cont.*)

1919	The **Nurses Act** established the first register for nurses; asylum attendants ('mental nurses') and male nurses were allowed to join only a supplementary part of this register.
1948	Establishment of the **National Health Service (NHS)**, which played a significant role in the development of nursing (but nurse education and the role of the nurse were slow to evolve)
1960s	Graduate-level nursing was first offered by the universities of Edinburgh and Manchester; the **Salmon Report** (1967) recommended developments for the nursing profession.
1970s	The decade saw a move away from training towards professional education, accompanied by the development of research into all aspects of education and practice; the **Briggs Committee on Nursing** (1972) recommended changes to education and regulation, including a widening of degree-level recruitment and a move towards making nursing a research-based profession; the University of Manchester appointed the first Chair of Nursing, Jean McFarlane, in 1974.
1980s	'**Project 2000**' (**P2K**) was established; the aim of P2K was to ensure that all nurses were educated in universities rather than trained in hospitals by the year 2000; P2K was successfully completed in the late 1990s.
2002	Establishment of the **Nursing and Midwifery Council (NMC)**
2010	Introduction of legislation in England (slightly earlier in Scotland, Wales and Northern Ireland) which decreed that all nurses must be educated to degree level

Reflection

Which of the events or developments in Table 3.1 do you think have had the most impact on nursing today? Why?

The Nursing and Midwifery Code ('The Code')

The Nursing and Midwifery Council (NMC) continues to work to '*maintain the register, provide educational guidance and ensure protection of the public*' (Lee-Woolf et al, 2015, p 7). The NMC Code enshrines the values and the legal and ethical principles which have emerged as part of the historical development outlined in Table 3.1. It outlines professional standards which are fundamental to good nursing practice:

The Code contains the professional standards that registered nurses and midwives must uphold. UK nurses and midwives must act in line with the Code, whether they are providing direct care to individuals, groups or communities or bringing their professional knowledge to bear on nursing and midwifery practice in other roles, such as leadership, education and research. While you can interpret the values and principles set out in the Code in a range of different practice settings, they are not negotiable or discretionary.

(NMC, 2015, p 2)

Reflection

1) Consider some of the values and principles outlined in the NMC Code (2015) listed below. Can you think of everyday situations where nurses need to put each of these things into practice?

   a) Preserving the dignity of patients

   b) Treating people with kindness, respect and compassion

   c) Practising safely

   d) Communicating clearly to patients and colleagues

   e) Promoting professionalism and trust

   f) Upholding people's human rights

   g) Challenging poor practice

   h) Challenging discrimination

2) How do the following relate to these values and principles?

   a) Making sure that an elderly patient can reach her water cup

   b) Making sure that a vegetarian patient has been given information on suitable food choices

   c) Ensuring that a patient's 'next of kin' is determined by the patient, and not by blood or marital status where the patient has the capacity to make that decision

   d) Asking children and young people, and not just their parents, for views about any care or treatment they are involved in

   e) Making large-print material available for those who have a visual impairment

   f) Making pictorial or other appropriate material available for those with a learning disability, so they are aware of what treatment might mean

Current developments in nursing

The NMC Code provides a core framework for professional practice. However, nursing continues to evolve as medical and nursing knowledge advances and social expectations and constraints impact on the profession. These changes are reflected in updates to the NMC Code. In fact, nursing is currently undergoing an unprecedented rate of change, some positive, some challenging and potentially problematic. Examples include (Lee-Woolf et al, 2015; Pryjmachuk, 2011): changes in how users access services; the introduction of competition and the free market in the provision of services; advances in treatments and technologies; ever-increasing public scrutiny; changes to the power balance between patient and professional, especially in mental health care, with aspirations that all care should be 'co-produced', ie genuinely planned and agreed jointly by patients and their key healthcare workers.

In this constantly evolving climate, the maintenance of professional standards requires the development and constant updating of knowledge and skills relating to a wide range of subjects including (Lee-Woolf et al, 2015): anatomy; physiology; microbiology; psychology; sociology; health education; pharmacology; law and ethics; communication. For specialist nurses, duties can involve additional responsibilities such as prescribing drugs and performing minor surgery (Isaac, 2015; Lee-Woolf et al, 2015). Professionalism also requires a respect for evidence-based practice, as well as an understanding of the theories which underpin it, and the official policies which govern it.

Reflective practice

Reflective practice entails the critical analysis of your own experiences and actions in order to improve future performance. It is particularly important in practice-based professional learning contexts like nursing, where it can allow practitioners to make meaningful connections between theory and practice and facilitate continuous learning in an ever-changing context.

Reflective practice is an important way of helping nurses inform their day-to-day decision making and clinical judgement.

Your professional portfolio

The cornerstone of reflective practice is a nurse's professional **portfolio** (sometimes called a 'profile'). A portfolio is a collection of materials associated with an individual's learning experiences and achievements. It is an integral element of continuing professional development (CPD) and lifelong learning. It may be required for assessment and employment purposes, and for nurses, it can provide important evidence for Accreditation of Prior Experiential Learning (APEL) and for NMC revalidation purposes.

A portfolio can include course handbooks, certificates, copies of assessments and feedback from a variety of sources (those who mark your assignments, your peers, your mentors and supervisors and the patients and service users you care for, for example). Portfolios should not be mere repositories of information (ie a folder full of certificates and assessments); they need to demonstrate some degree of critical analysis and reflection on those aspects of learning important to you. Hence, good portfolios always contain reflections (eg individual reflective accounts, reflective journals or situational analyses of events and incidents that were critical to your learning).

CROSS REFERENCE

Chapter 1, Studying nursing in higher education, APEL; Lifelong learning

Identifying and challenging poor practice

Reflective practice applies to what you observe around you, as well as to your own actions. As public-facing workers, nurses have a particular responsibility to be aware of any behaviour which may damage patients, other staff, or the reputation of the NHS or other care providers.

Most people have a story which is testament to the professionalism of nurses and the humanitarian values which underpin their actions – tales of how kind the nurses were to an elderly relative, or of the sensitivity shown to a distressed friend or family member receiving bad news. However, a quick perusal of the media also reveals some negative and disturbing reports, particularly with regard to the care received by the elderly and those with learning disabilities. Public investigations into poor practice, such as the Francis Report (Francis, 2013) on care failings in Mid Staffordshire, and the Mazars Report (Mazars, 2015) on the failure to investigate unexpected deaths at Southern Health, an NHS mental healthcare provider, inevitably lead to periods of professional introspection regarding core values. Nurses are considered as partners with other health professionals and service users, and this necessitates the ability to identify and the willingness to challenge any problematic practice or behaviour they witness, albeit '*in a constructive and helpful way*' (Lee-Woolf et al, 2015, p 12).

Reflection

Being critical means not only dissecting an event, situation or piece of writing etc for faults; it also means identifying strengths or learning opportunities from that event, situation or piece of writing etc.

With reference to the values and principles of the NMC Code (2015) outlined earlier, what do you think nurses could learn from scandals such as those at Mid Staffordshire and Southern Health? Think particularly about:

- challenging poor practice;
- promoting trust (through transparency and honesty);
- communicating effectively (to the public not just patients);
- safe practice.

CROSS REFERENCE

Chapter 4, Critical thinking

Graduate attributes

Belonging to a particular community entails developing in a way that is valued by that community. UK universities have stated a commitment to fostering certain attributes which it is believed students should possess when they graduate. These **graduate attributes** have been defined as *'the skills, knowledge and abilities of university graduates, beyond disciplinary knowledge, which are applicable to a range of contexts'* (Barrie, 2004, p 262). They relate to the following areas:

Figure 3.1: Graduate attributes (adapted from Hounsell, 2011, pp 2–3)

Reflection

Do you agree that these are the most important attributes that a graduate should demonstrate?

Do you think there are any important attributes missing from the list?

Task

- Which graduate attributes could be developed in the following activities? How?
  1) Giving a group presentation
  2) Completing a dissertation
  3) Contributing to an internet forum on nursing issues
  4) Becoming familiar with the NMC Code
  5) Finding and subsequently attending a library workshop on developing PowerPoint skills
  6) Actively managing your online presence (Facebook, Twitter, Instagram, LinkedIn etc)
  7) Carefully proofreading your essay
  8) Reading a quality newspaper (paper or online) on a regular basis
  9) Becoming a course representative in your department
  10) Learning a language

Discussion: applying graduate attributes

1) Giving a group presentation involves collaborative preparation and planning, working in teams with other students. It might also be necessary for you to take on a leadership role if you have knowledge or experience which others do not (*collaboration, teamwork and leadership*). As teamwork and leadership are highly valued in the workplace, you will be enhancing your own employability (*employability and career development*). In order to prepare your presentation, you will need to draw on and develop your research and communication skills (*research, scholarship and enquiry; communication and information literacy*).

2) Completing a dissertation requires autonomy (*personal and intellectual autonomy*) and advanced research skills (*research, scholarship and enquiry*), including command of technological resources (*communication and information literacy*). Academic writing is a key communication skill (*communication and information literacy*) which will also prepare you for formal communication in the workplace, thus enhancing your employability (*employability and career development*).

3) Contributing to an internet forum on nursing issues is a form of collaboration (*collaboration, teamwork and leadership*) and a way of exploring social and professional understanding (*ethical, social and professional understanding*). It also develops a particular set of communication skills related to social networking which could extend to a global scale (*communication and information literacy; global citizenship*).

4) Becoming familiar with the NMC Code is primarily a way of extending professional understanding for academic and workplace purposes (*ethical, social and professional understanding; employability and career development*).

5) Finding and subsequently attending a library workshop on developing PowerPoint skills displays personal autonomy (*personal and intellectual autonomy*) and a commitment to improving your communication skills (*communication and information literacy; lifelong learning*). PowerPoint is also a skill valued by employers (*employability and career development*).

6) Actively managing your online presence (Facebook, Twitter, Instagram, LinkedIn etc) allows you to be in control of how you are viewed by potential employers and colleagues (*communication and information literacy; employability and career development*).

7) Carefully proofreading your essay indicates a commitment to developing your written communication skills (*communication and information literacy*). This will be valued in academia and in the workplace (*employability and career development*).

8) Reading a quality newspaper (paper or online) on a regular basis can be a way of keeping up to date with social and global issues (*ethical, social and professional understanding*), which can in turn help you to understand and respond to workplace issues (*employability and career development*).

9) Becoming a course representative in your academic department can help you build on your communication and leadership skills (*communication and information literacy; collaboration, teamwork and leadership*). This is something that might catch the eye of a prospective employer if included on your CV (*employability and career development*).

10) Learning a language is a way of achieving cultural understanding, and of enhancing your skill set in an increasingly internationalised workplace (*global citizenship; lifelong learning*).

Top tips

Standing out to prospective employers

Be sure to add activities like those discussed above to your CV, as the graduate attributes they demonstrate are of great interest to employers. Evidence of such attributes could make you stand out in a competitive employment market.

Summary

This chapter has explored the ways in which you can become a member of your academic community. It has discussed the values and principles which underpin university life and the foundations of nursing. It has detailed some of the practices and conventions which govern both academic life, and nursing education and practice. It has also introduced the concept of graduate attributes, and examined their importance in terms of employability.

References

Academic Phrasebank [online]. Available at: www.phrasebank.manchester.ac.uk/ (accessed 16 March 2017).

Baily, S (2014) *Academic Writing: A Handbook for International Students*. 4th ed. Abingdon: Routledge.

Barrie, S (2004) A Research-based Approach to Generic Graduate Attributes Policy. *Higher Education Research & Development*, 23(3): 261–75.

Becher, T (1989) *Academic Tribes and Territories: Intellectual Enquiry and the Culture of Disciplines*. Buckingham: Society for Research in Higher Education and Open University Press.

Bottomley, J (2014) *Academic Writing for International Students of Science*. Abingdon: Routledge.

Francis, R (2013) *Report of the Mid Staffordshire NHS Foundation Trust Public Inquiry*. London: The Stationery Office.

Hounsell, D (2011) *Graduates for the 21st Century: Integrating the Enhancement Themes*. Glasgow: The Quality Assurance Agency for Higher Education, pp 2–3.

Isaac, A (2015) History of Nursing – Timeline. Healthcare Network, Workforce Development. *The Guardian* [online]. Available at: www.theguardian.com/healthcare-network/ng-interactive/2015/sep/15/history-of-nursing-timeline (accessed 16 March 2017).

Lee-Woolf, E, Jones, J, Brooks, J and Timpson, J (2015) Essentials of Nursing: Values, Knowledge, Skills and Practice, in Burns, D (ed) *Foundations of Adult Nursing*. London: Sage.

Mazars (2015) *Independent Review of Deaths of People with a Learning Disability or Mental Health Problem in Contact with Southern Health NHS Foundation Trust April 2011 to March 2015*. London: Mazars LLP.

NMC (Nursing and Midwifery Council) (2015) *The Code: Professional Standards of Practice and Behaviour for Nurses and Midwives* [online]. Available at: www.nmc.org.uk/globalassets/sitedocuments/nmc-publications/nmc-code.pdf (accessed 16 March 2017).

Pryjmachuk, S (ed) (2011) *Mental Health Nursing: An Evidence-Based Introduction*. London: Sage.

Swales, J (1990) *Genre Analysis*. Cambridge: Cambridge University Press.

Swales, J and Feak, C (2012) *Academic Writing for Graduate Students: Essential Tasks and Skills*. 3rd ed. Michigan: Michigan ELT.

Chapter 4
Critical thinking

Learning outcomes

After reading this chapter you will:
- understand what is meant by the term 'critical';
- have gained an understanding of what it means to think critically;
- have developed a critical approach to learning and the use of resources;
- have acquired some strategies for reading critically;
- have acquired some strategies for writing, and presenting work, critically.

Critical thinking lies at the heart of academic life and is essential for academic success. As a university student, you will be expected to take a critical approach to all your learning activities and assessment tasks. This chapter introduces the concept of critical thinking and explores its application in the acquisition and reporting of information and ideas, as well as in clinical nursing practice. The ideas in this chapter are discussed in further detail in the *Critical Thinking* book in the Critical Study Skills series.

What is critical thinking?

You will encounter the word 'critical' frequently in university life: you may be asked to *write critically* in an essay, or to *critically review* a journal article; you may receive feedback on an essay which says it is not *critical* enough, that you need to adopt a more *critical approach*; there may be modules on your course with titles such as *Critical Thinking*, and the course descriptions of other modules may mention the importance of *criticality*, *critical reading skills* and *critical writing skills*. It is clear that being *critical* is important in academic life. But what do academics mean when they use this word?

Reflection

- Look at the entry for 'critical' in the *Chambers 21st Century Dictionary*. Which of the definitions do you think most reflects the way academics would usually use this word? Which, for you, is the most 'normal' use in day-to-day life? Which definition is of particular relevance to nurses in clinical practice?

> **critical** /'krɪtɪkəl/ ⊳ *adj* **1** fault-finding; disapproving. **2** relating to a critic or criticism. **3** involving analysis and assessment. **4** relating to a crisis; decisive; crucial. **5** urgent; vital. **6** said of a patient: so ill or seriously injured as to be at risk of dying. **7** *physics* denoting a state, level or value at which there is a significant change in the properties of a system □ *critical mass* □ *critical temperature*. **8** *nuclear physics* said of a fissionable material, a nuclear reactor, etc: having reached the point at which a nuclear chain reaction is self-sustaining. ● **critically** *adverb*. ● **criticality** *noun*. ● **criticalness** *noun*.

When you are asked at university to do something in a 'critical' way, it is normally the third use, involving 'analysis and assessment' (Chambers), which is meant. Other dictionary definitions include the related terms 'evaluation' (Oxford Dictionaries), or 'judgement' (Merriam-Webster). This use of the word is different from the most common use of the word in everyday life, ie 'fault-finding' or 'disapproving'; however, negative judgements can of course form part of general evaluation – a critical review of an article will discuss weaknesses as well as strengths. Criticising in this sense is certainly part of critical thinking, but it is not central. The sixth use, describing the condition of a patient, is less common, but obviously very relevant to nursing practice.

Since academics frequently use the term 'critical' in conjunction with 'analyse' and 'evaluate', or imply these things in their use of the word 'critical', it is important to understand precisely what they mean by these words. To explore this, it is helpful to step outside the academic world and consider for a moment your wider everyday life.

Reflection

- Consider the questions below.
  1) Why did you decide to become a nurse?
  2) How did you choose a particular university for your studies?
  3) Where do you get your news about the world? Why?
  4) Who is your favourite writer? Why?
  5) Is your diet healthy? Why/why not?
  6) How did you choose what to wear this morning?

In order to answer the reflection questions, you had to **analyse** by examining certain things in a detailed and systematic way, breaking them down into their constituent parts. You might have:

- looked at a range of different occupations in terms of how interesting they appear, the knowledge and skills required, and the degree to which they match your own personality and skills;
- categorised universities according to region, type or reputation;
- distinguished newspapers or news websites according to their readability and/or political allegiances;
- identified the characteristics which distinguish a particular writer;
- assigned foods to different groups such as proteins, carbohydrates and fats;
- identified typical weather in the region in which you live.

The questions also require you to **evaluate**, ie *to make judgements*. You may do this to some extent on a personal, subjective level:

- you may feel you have a vocation to be a nurse;
- you may have chosen your university partly because you like a particular city or have family commitments there;
- your personal politics are likely to influence your choice of news outlet;
- your interest in particular topics and your taste in writing style will determine which authors appeal to you;
- your sense of individual style may influence the way you dress.

CROSS
REFERENCE

Stance

However, you might also base your judgements on **objective criteria** and **independent evidence** such as published university league tables, established scientific consensus on nutrition, or the evidence-based predictions of trained meteorologists ('weather scientists').

Critical analysis and evaluation enables you to provide **valid reasons** for your judgements and the decisions based on them, and this is a very important part of critical academic discourse. Instead of stating 'I believe such-and-such', or 'I just know such-and-such to be right', in critical academic discourse, you are required to provide an **evidenced-based rationale** for your views and beliefs.

There is no doubt that critical thinking is a difficult, abstract concept, but, as you can see, it is clearly not something mysterious or peculiar to universities. The examples you have reflected on show that critical thinking is in no way disconnected from everyday life: people use their critical faculties every day to form opinions and make decisions. The challenge for you as a new university student is to be aware of your existing, hopefully well-formed and well-practised critical faculties, and to apply them to a new academic context. Of course, there is always room to learn and develop, and being a university student will provide you with a unique opportunity to refine and extend your critical thinking skills, and, crucially, to demonstrate them in your nursing studies and assessments. The advanced critical thinking skills you develop at university are themselves transferable: you will go on to apply them in nursing practice and many other areas of life.

The critical thinker

Reflection

- Below are some adjectives which could describe a critical thinker:

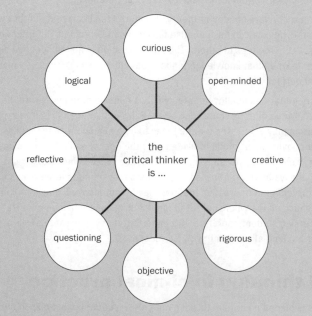

Figure 4.1: Qualities of the critical thinker

1) In what way do you think each of these qualities makes a person critical?
2) Try to think of a recent example in your family, study or work life when you demonstrated (or failed to demonstrate!) each of these qualities.
3) Which of these qualities is reflected in the following?

- Checking facts and claims in an article with reliable independent sources
- Considering issues or problems from different angles
- Gathering facts and ideas from a number of different sources and comparing them
- Comparing contrasting viewpoints
- Finding up-to-date examples which support or challenge particular viewpoints

Critical thinking in universities

CROSS
REFERENCE

Chapter 3,
Becoming
a member
of your
academic and
professional
community,
Teaching,
research and
knowledge,
Advanced
skills,
Research
reports

Critical thinking underpins the development of **knowledge** in universities. Your lecturers at university are also scholars engaged in the advancement of knowledge, and part of their job is to put forward **ideas** about what is going on in the world. These ideas come about in many ways: they often arise by means of previous work conducted on the subject by other scholars; they may come from direct observation of the world; they may be the result of a 'hunch' a person has (though even hunches usually owe something to previous work done by others – no one works in a vacuum!). In academia, these ideas are usually termed **theories** or **hypotheses**. Unlike facts, these ideas are not certain, and they must be investigated and tested through formal **research** if they are to have a chance of being accepted by the academic community. A particular theory or hypothesis gives rise to a **research question**, which scholars investigate, finding **evidence** along the way to support their ideas. Scholars present their research in a variety of ways, but the main vehicle is the **academic journal**. Scholars trust journal articles because, unlike some other sources, notably the internet, the research articles in them are critically reviewed by other respected scholars, ie they are said to be **peer reviewed**. However, this does not mean that readers can automatically accept the findings and conclusions put forward in journal articles: they must still review the ideas and evidence put forward *critically* to make sure they are credible.

As one scholar puts forward an idea or theory, it is more than likely that another will put forward an alternative one. They may do this because they view the world in a different way, or because they spot 'holes' in the theories of others. The latter situation is not as negative as it might sound. In Chapter 3, you learned that knowledge tends to advance in small steps; it does not suddenly appear, fully and perfectly formed!

CROSS
REFERENCE

Chapter 3,
Becoming
a member
of your
academic and
professional
community,
Teaching,
research and
knowledge

Every new theory generates healthy debate, which is necessary to make sure that ideas are rigorously tested. Much of this debate is conducted through academic journals, but conferences and other platforms play a part. The debate tends to be 'won' by the side that has the most substantive and convincing portfolio of evidence or the one whose arguments best fit the data *at a given point in time*. This proviso is important: just because something is right *now*, does not mean it will always be right! More and better data may be uncovered which points to other conclusions; more efficient or creative theories may be put forward; a new and unexpected discovery may shake up the whole field – although this is not a common occurrence. As you progress as a nursing student, therefore, it is important that you learn to explore alternative viewpoints, approaching all research with a critical eye.

Critical thinking in clinical practice

CROSS
REFERENCE

Chapter 3,
Becoming
a member
of your
academic and
professional
community,
Reflective
practice

Great emphasis is placed on critical thinking not only in education, but also in nursing practice. Critical thinking underpins the notion of **reflective practice**, which is central to the nursing profession. Reflective practice is essentially the critical analysis of your own behaviours and thoughts while you practise as a nurse, in order to improve your future practice. It involves analysing situations and events that go well or not so well. Reflective practice clearly relates to curiosity, open-mindedness and questioning (Figure 4.1); indeed, one of the most well-known tools for helping practitioners reflect consists of three simple questions (Borton, 1970):

- *What?*
- *So what?*
- *Now what?*

Critical thinking also underpins **evidence-based practice**, an approach to healthcare practice that requires nurses, doctors and other healthcare practitioners to analyse and evaluate the evidence associated with their current and future practices. For example, while washing hands might be 'common sense' in the prevention of hospital-acquired infections, the critical thinking nurse understands that it is not simply hand-washing that is important, but what the literature and research says about the frequency and method of hand-washing, and the types of cleansers used. The World

Health Organisation has an evidence-based approach to hand hygiene called 'Five Moments' that not only focuses on the times ('the when') nurses and other healthcare professionals should wash their hands, but also provides, in each case, a rationale (the 'why') (see Sax et al, 2007 for more detail).

CROSS REFERENCE

Demonstrating criticality in your clinical practice

Applying and developing your critical thinking skills

As a student nurse, it is important to take a critical approach to every aspect of your studies and clinical practice. You should be critical in the way you approach tasks, use sources of information, and present your work and ideas, both in your study activities, and in written, oral and practical assessments.

Approaching learning resources critically

As a university student, you will find information and ideas in many sources, the main ones being lectures, textbooks and academic journals. Lectures are delivered by people who are authorities in the field. Textbooks and academic journals are trusted because they are peer reviewed. Other sources, such as the media, websites, blogs, videos and podcasts may also be useful in certain contexts, but these should be used with extreme care, as it is harder to assess their credibility.

Taking a critical approach to source use means taking time to assess the relevance, credibility and authority of each particular source. Below are some questions which will help you to do this:

- Who wrote or created it? If it was a 'corporate' author (an organisation rather than a person writing the source), is that organisation credible?
- Are the authors considered to be an authority in the field?
- Do they have a relevant professional affiliation?
- Are they cited by scholars in other books and articles?
- What is the publication date?
- Is it the latest edition of a book?
- Are there more recent sources which may advance or question the content?
- Who is the intended reader or listener?
- What is the scope of the work?
- Is it published by an educational publisher or in a reputable academic journal?

Task

- Look at the following sources and decide if they are credible sources for student nurses:
  1) Burns, D (ed) (2015) *Foundations of Adult Nursing*. London: Sage.
  2) Pryjmachuk, S (ed) (2011) *Mental Health Nursing: An Evidence-based Introduction*. London: Sage.
  3) Etheridge, K (2004) Recognising and Responding to Adolescents with Mental Illness. *Primary Health Care*, 14: 36–41.
  4) Southgate, J, Mital, D and Stock, A (2008) Are Women from High-risk Ethnic Minority Groups More Likely to Decline HIV Screening? *International Journal of STD & AIDS*, 19: 206–7.
  5) Independent Mental Health Taskforce to the NHS in England (2016) *The Five Year Forward View for Mental Health* [online]. Available at: www.england.nhs.uk/mentalhealth/taskforce/ (accessed 17 March 2017).
  6) Royal College of Nursing (2014) *Nutrition in Children and Young People with Cancer: RCN Guidance*. London: RCN.
  7) Boots' WebMD website [online]. Available at: www.webmd.boots.com (accessed 17 March 2017).
  8) The StudentNurse.net website and forums [online]. Available at: https://studentnurse.net/ (accessed 17 March 2017).

Discussion: identifying academic sources

(1) and (2) are established research- and evidence-based textbooks used across nursing departments in universities.

(3) and (4) are articles published in reputable, peer-reviewed academic journals. There has been an explosion in less-than-reputable journals – including nursing and healthcare journals – in the last few years, especially online, and it can be hard to tell if a journal is reputable or not. There are many so-called 'predatory publishers' around, whose reputations are poor because they do not adhere to the standards associated with more reputable journals (rigorous peer review, screening of expert board members etc). If in doubt, you can ask your lecturers or your university library for advice.

'Corporate' authors have written documents (5) and (6). In both cases, the authors are reputable and credible organisations: the Independent Taskforce (5) was set up by the NHS in England, and the Royal College of Nursing (6) is a well-known professional nursing organisation.

While Boots (7) is a reputable consumer pharmacy, it is a commercial operation whose principal business is selling health and beauty products, and thus there is no guarantee that its advice will be unbiased. The forums on StudentNurse.net (8) might be very interesting and useful to you as a student, but they will be filled largely with subjective advice and opinions, so they will be of little use as an academic source.

CROSS REFERENCE

Chapter 5, Academic resources: technology and the library, The university library, Knowing what's out there

Top tips

Choosing the right source

Academic books include textbooks, edited collections, monographs (in-depth analyses of a subject), and reference works such as medical dictionaries. **Textbooks** (some of which are edited collections of chapters by different authors) are a good source of information and facts, and they are also useful in that they can provide an overview of the discipline (eg midwifery) or topic (eg home birth). They often summarise the way knowledge has developed in a certain area of nursing or medicine, sketching out the background and presenting the arguments that have been advanced along the way.

Journal articles often present a particular argument, usually through the reporting of a piece of research, with conclusions based on the results of that research. These journal articles will refer to other studies in order to provide a context for the current work. Some journal articles are 'review' articles, whose aim is to compare and contrast all the main studies that have been carried out in a particular area so as to identify any general tendencies or issues. Some journal articles are opinion pieces, but these are less common.

Active reading

Reading firstly requires you to actively engage any prior knowledge you have on a topic. This entails reflecting on what you already know or believe, and then looking out for particular things as you read. You need to be ready to notice anything interesting or important. Begin by asking yourself two questions:

- Why are you reading?
- What do you expect/hope to find out?

Looking at the items in Table 4.1 may help you determine to what extent the source will provide answers to your questions.

Table 4.1: Understanding the gist of books and articles

BOOK	JOURNAL ARTICLE
Title	Title
Blurb on the back cover	Abstract
Information about the author(s) (so you can check their credibility)	Information about the author(s) (so you can check their credibility)
Contents page	Headings and sub-headings
Introduction	Introduction
Chapter aims or learning outcomes listed at the start of each chapter (as in this book)	Figures and Tables (which visually summarise the evidence)
Conclusion	Discussion/Conclusion
Index	

Once you have identified a source as potentially useful, the next step in active reading usually involves taking notes or highlighting important information. However you do this, you should be systematic in your approach, as this can save time and effort later on.

Synthesis of information and ideas

At the beginning of your undergraduate studies, you will be required to demonstrate your *understanding* of dominant theories or important studies. As you progress, you will be expected to show an increasing awareness of alternative viewpoints on a topic and of the importance of evidence in evaluating them. As you do this, you need to find ways of categorising and *synthesising* information and ideas. For example, if you are reading to find out about the main treatment pathways for depression, it might be useful if you create a table or database like the one below.

Table 4.2: Treatment pathways for depression

TREATMENTS FOR DEPRESSION	TYPE OF EVIDENCE	ROLE OF THE NURSE	STUDIES / REFERENCES	KEY FINDINGS
Anti-depressants	National guidance	Knowledge of treatment effects and side effects	National Institute for Health and Clinical Excellence (2016) *Depression in Adults: Recognition and Management [Clinical guideline CG90].* London: NICE	Do not use anti-depressants for subthreshold depressive symptoms or mild depression; useful in moderate–severe depression when combined with CBT

Table 4.2: (*cont.*)

TREATMENTS FOR DEPRESSION	TYPE OF EVIDENCE	ROLE OF THE NURSE	STUDIES / REFERENCES	KEY FINDINGS
	Cochrane Review		Arroll, B, et al (2009) Antidepressants versus Placebo for Depression in Primary Care. *Cochrane Database of Systematic Reviews*, Issue 3. Art. No.: CD007954	Fourteen studies examined in which tricyclic or SSRI anti-depressants were compared against a placebo control; results show that most anti-depressants were effective for depression; most of the studies were supported by funds from pharmaceutical companies
Problem-solving	Research study	Nurses delivered the treatment	Kendrick, T et al (2005) A Trial of Problem-solving by Community Mental Health Nurses for Anxiety, Depression and Life Difficulties among General Practice Patients. The CPN-GP Study. *Health Technology Assessment*, 9(37): 1–104	Specialist mental health nurse as good as support from GPs for patients with anxiety, depression and reactions to life difficulties, but more expensive
Cognitive-Behaviour Therapy (CBT)	Systematic review and meta-analysis (see also NICE guidance above)	Some nurses are also trained as CBT therapists	Linde, K et al (2015) Effectiveness of Psychological Treatments for Depressive Disorders in Primary Care: Systematic Review and Meta-analysis. *Annals of Family Medicine*, 13(1): 56–68	Psychological treatments are effective; for CBT, there is substantial evidence that treatments that are less resource-intensive are as good as more intense treatments

Table 4.2: (*cont.*)

TREATMENTS FOR DEPRESSION	TYPE OF EVIDENCE	ROLE OF THE NURSE	STUDIES / REFERENCES	KEY FINDINGS
Physical exercise	Research report from a reputable mental health charity	Nurses can facilitate exercise in people with depression	Mental Health Foundation (2007) *Up and Running? Exercise Therapy and the Treatment of Mild–Moderate Depression in Primary Care.* London: MHF	Lots of evidence to show that physical exercise is an effective treatment for mild to moderate depression but it is unlikely to be prescribed by GPs

As you gather information and ideas in this way, you should do so with a critical eye. Active, critical reading may involve:

- identifying developments in knowledge and thinking among scholars;
- comparing and contrasting ideas, theories and findings;
- identifying shared or contrasting views and the reasoning behind them;
- identifying, examining and evaluating evidence;
- comparing the scope of different studies;
- comparing the conclusions of different studies;
- discerning relationships and patterns, and things which do not seem to 'fit in' with everything else;
- relating ideas, theories and research to your existing knowledge and the current context, eg the essay question in hand.

Advanced skills

CROSS REFERENCE

Academic Writing and Referencing, Chapter 3, Referring to sources

Originality

Originality is part of critical thinking, which becomes more important as you advance in your studies, so it is important to understand what is meant by 'original' in academia. It is unusual to be original in the sense of spontaneously coming up with an entirely new idea in academia, but a new perspective on how things relate to each other is a valid example of original thought. This treatment of information and ideas is a type of '*knowledge **transformation**'*, as opposed to the simpler process of '*knowledge **telling**'* (Beireiter and Scardamalia, 1987). These concepts will be further explored in *Academic Writing and Referencing*, as the relationship between criticality, intelligent use of sources, and originality is examined.

Scrutinising research and arguments

A great deal of academic discourse is devoted to putting forward arguments. When reading or listening to these arguments, you need to isolate and identify the author's line of reasoning, and then evaluate it according to clear criteria.

- Is the argument clearly articulated, for example in the introduction to a book or article? Is this reflected in the content of the book or article?
- Is the argument developed in a logical way? Is it based on sound reasoning? Does each stage of the argument follow on logically from the next? Does everything *make sense*?
- Is there sufficient evidence to support the argument? Is it credible and convincing? Does it lead naturally to the conclusion, or could other valid conclusions be drawn?
- Have alternative viewpoints and possibilities been explored?

LIBRARY, UNIVERSITY OF CHESTER

Adopting a critical approach means looking out for anything which might weaken the argument you are listening to or reading. There are certain terms which may help you to critique an argument (some of which are sometimes used by lecturers when they critique (mark) assessments).

Task

 Match the terms on the left with the correct definition on the right. (The first one has been done as an example.)

Premise	A reason for doing something which is often not directly declared
Assumption	Not supported by facts
Agenda	Ideas on which subsequent ideas or actions are based
Anecdotal	Something which is accepted as true without question or proof
Bias	The action of supporting or opposing someone or something in an unfair way, allowing personal opinion to influence your judgement
Subjective	Based on personal experience rather than research
Unsubstantiated	Based on personal beliefs and feelings, rather than on facts

Reflection

1) Look at the claims below and decide if there is anything which weakens them. For example:
   - Are there any false premises?
   - Is there any bias?
   - Is the argument subjective?
   - Is the argument unbalanced?
   - Could the writer/speaker have an agenda?
   - Is the data reliable?
   - Is there is any evidence which is purely anecdotal?
   - Are assertions, appeals etc based on emotional appeal or personal anecdote rather than logical reasoning?
   - Are there are any assumptions, overgeneralisations or unsubstantiated claims?
   - Is there any inconsistency or ambiguity?
   - Is there any flawed reasoning?
   a) Ten years ago, 20 per cent of students got the top grade in their exam. Now, 40 per cent do. This proves that exams are getting easier.
   b) Poor families suffer from comparatively greater ill health because they eat unhealthily, and smoke and drink too much.
   c) It is clear that smoking marijuana causes people to crave stronger drugs like cocaine and heroin, as statistics show that almost all people who become addicted to hard drugs smoked marijuana first.
   d) All people become forgetful as they get older. It happened to all my grandparents.

e) People from different backgrounds can't live together harmoniously in the same neighbourhood. Almost everyone I've talked to thinks the same way. We all feel very strongly about it.

f) Research proves that providing information to patients about an operation reduces post-operative pain.

g) I use my mobile all the time and I've never had any problems, so clearly there are no health risks involved.

2) Identify some examples of problematic language use, for example, incautious expression such as 'proves' in a).

If an argument or theory is reported in a journal article or conference paper, there are particular questions you should bear in mind as you read:

- Are the writers qualified to carry out the research? Are they authorities on the subject? What is their professional role? Do they have any vested interests?
- What are the objectives of the study? Are they clearly articulated?
- What is the problem or 'gap' in the knowledge that the study addresses?
- What is the hypothesis or research question behind the study?
- Do the writers provide sufficient context and lay the ground for their research question?
- Is the relevant literature reviewed?
- Is the methodology sound? Could it be reproduced by other scholars?
- Are the interpretations of the results credible?
- Have the implications of the study for nursing practice been correctly identified?
- Have the limitations of the study been acknowledged?
- Has the study advanced knowledge in the field of nursing?

Task

 Look at the following extract from the introduction to a published journal article (Pryjmachuk et al, 2011) and see how many of the above questions you can answer. (You would need to access the full article online to answer *all* the questions.)

Introduction

Mental health problems in children and young people are a major public health issue. In the UK, as many as one in five children and young people will experience developmental, emotional or behavioural problems and approximately ten per cent will have a mental disorder that meets diagnostic criteria (Green et al 2005).

As mental health problems in the general population frequently commence in adolescence (Kessler et al 2005), there is a strong case for embedding the skills of recognition and basic management into wider health and education services. Indeed, school-based services for early identification and intervention and for care coordination in primary care are advocated in the USA (Taras 2004) and in many other European countries (Braddick et al 2009).

In the UK, child and adolescent mental health service provision ('CAMHS') exists under the auspices of a four-tier model that reflects increasing levels of specialisation and case complexity. Tier 1 encompasses anyone working in universal children's services (including teachers and school nurses); Tier 2 workers are the unidisciplinary specialists (such as psychologists) working in primary and community-oriented care; Tier 3 services are provided mainly by multidisciplinary teams working in outpatient (sometimes day care) services; Tier 4 provision – which equates largely with hospitalisation – is for the minority with the most complex needs (CAMHS Review, 2008). Primary-oriented care and community-oriented care are thus an inherent part of CAMHS, yet this provision is often overlooked. For many, CAMHS is synonymous with Tiers 3 and 4 or, at the very least, it begins at Tier 2. These higher tier services are often overstretched, with many having long waiting lists (Clarke et al 2003, Etheridge

2004, CAMHS Review 2008). Moreover, in-patient (Tier 4) services are expensive, both for the service provider and for the families receiving the service (Jacobs et al 2004).

There have been calls to enhance service provision at the lower tiers (NHS HAS 1995, Audit Commission 1999, CAMHS Review 2008). Schools often feature in these calls: they are, after all, rooted in the community and are a normal part of childhood. Indeed, Appleton (2000) argues that schools are primary care CAMHS provision. However, while schools certainly have the potential to improve children's mental health, there is little clarity over who should take the lead. Those earmarked for the job have tended to be education rather than health professionals – teachers, school counsellors and educational psychologists, for example – and while few would question the need for interdisciplinary collaboration in children's services, it is odd not to see health professionals taking a lead on what is essentially a health issue.

Of the health professionals who could take the lead, school nurses are a natural choice. Unlike specialist CAMHS workers, they are part of the normal experience of growing up and are consequently more accessible and less stigmatising. They are a key aspect of universal health services, and surveys and consultations in the UK and elsewhere indicate that they have considerable involvement in identifying and addressing mental health issues (DeBell 2006, Haddad et al 2010), an activity to which they would like to devote more time (Ball 2009).

Background

Reviews and guidelines from the UK (NICE 2005, 2008, 2009), other European nations (Stengård & Appelqvist-Schmidlechner 2010), Canada (Zuckerbrot et al 2007) and the USA (Olin & Hoagwood 2002, AACAP, 2009) recommend developing the capacity and quality of school- and primary care-based support for common mental disorders, with school nurses being key to this activity. However, there is relatively little research concerning school nurses and mental health work. Although studies have been conducted in the UK's constituent countries and in Sweden and France, most work in this area has been undertaken in the USA. Puskar and Bernardo (2007), Bullock et al (2002) and DeSocio et al (2006), for example, provide evidence that school nurses can be successfully involved in mental health screening, promotion and early intervention activities.

In the UK, Leighton et al (2003) undertook a small survey of school nurses together with a small-scale evaluation of a school nurse training programme in England, while Wilson et al (2008) undertook a larger survey of health visitors and school nurses in Scotland. Both studies found a wide range of mental health concerns in school nurse caseloads including major mental health problems like psychosis, self-harm and eating disorders. Three studies examined regular contact with CAMHS professionals: Richardson and Partridge (2000) evaluated the provision of monthly consultations by CAMHS professionals to school nurse teams; Clarke et al (2003) looked at the provision of psychologist-led monthly supervision and training sessions; and Chipman and Gooch (2003) examined a school-based, school nurse-led clinic for emotional and mental health issues that involved monthly supervision from CAMHS professionals. All three studies reported largely positive findings, as did Leighton et al's training programme. Moreover, in what is the closest to what might be called a patient outcome study, Stallard et al (2007) explored the potential of using school nurses to facilitate a cognitive-behavioural programme designed to improve children's emotional health, finding statistically significant and sustained improvements in anxiety and self-esteem among the children who took part.

While school nurses are well placed for primary care level mental health work with young people and while the literature details some efforts to develop, quantify and evaluate this aspect of their role, there are also indications that there may be difficulties engaging school nurses in such work – not necessarily through a lack of willingness but through a lack of confidence or limited relevant training (Leighton et al 2003, DeBell 2006, NISHYP 2006, Wilson et al 2008). Pressures on time and the demands of other important public health issues like sexual health and healthy eating may also be obstacles (Ball 2009). The aim of this study was therefore to explore the views of school nurses regarding mental health problems in young people and their potential for engaging in mental health work with this client group.

Demonstrating criticality in your academic work

So far, you have focused on how to think critically. However, it is not only important to *think* critically; you must know how to *demonstrate* your critical thinking in all your academic work, both through the content, and with careful use of language.

Discussion versus description

To demonstrate criticality in your work, there must be a high level of **discussion** throughout. To do this successfully, it is necessary to understand the difference between *description* and *discussion*, and to recognise these things in your reading, and in your own work.

Task

1) Look back at the introduction section of the article extract in the previous task and identify which parts of text are:
   - description;
   - discussion.
2) Which words and phrases helped you to recognise these two things?

As you write, or present work orally, you will usually move from description to discussion. As you progress through your undergraduate studies, you will be expected to engage in increasingly complex levels of discussion.

Increasing complexity

Description

- Presenting facts.

Discussion

- Demonstrating understanding of a topic through analysis and evaluation.
- Demonstrating understanding of debates and alternate viewpoints, and their associated evidence.
- Weighing up the evidence for one side or another.
- Revealing the implications of different aspects of your analysis and evaluation for your overall argument.
- Guiding the reader or listener through the process by which you arrived at your conclusions.

Figure 4.2: Levels of complexity in discussion

CROSS
REFERENCE

*Academic
Writing and
Referencing*

Stance

While it is important to include the views of scholars and authorities in your work, this must be as part of the wider primary objective, which is to say what *you* think. You need to feel able to let your own voice emerge. Your opinion, supported by research and evidence, is known as your **stance**, ie your position on the topic, what you believe, with good reason, to be true or correct. This becomes more important as you advance in your studies.

Adopting and maintaining a stance requires confidence. You need to feel secure in your understanding of the issues and your ability to persuade. There is no easy route to attaining this kind of confidence; it is something you will build over time and with experience. You may find that your stance is different from that of your lecturer. This is fine, as long as you present a clear rationale and evidence to support your view.

CROSS
REFERENCE

Chapter 2,
*Studying for
your Nursing
Degree*,
Working
independently,
working
in teams

CROSS
REFERENCE

*Academic
Writing and
Referencing*,
Chapter 1,
Academic
writing: text,
process and
criticality,
The writing
process

Top tips

Developing your stance

1) Test your understanding, ideas and opinions through discussion in study groups. Arrange to get together informally with other students to discuss important topics. This type of collaboration is a valid part of academic life: this is what your lecturers do when they network at conferences. Of course, you must be careful that it doesn't spill over into 'collusion' (ie working together in order to deceive), which counts as academic malpractice.

2) Start writing! Getting words down on paper is one of the best ways to clarify your own thinking. As you struggle with meaning and expression, you may reveal misunderstandings and gaps in your knowledge, and expose vague ideas and ambiguities. You can then go back to your lecture notes, books and articles, or talk to lecturers and fellow students, and try to clear things up. When you return to the page, you will hopefully be able to improve the content and expression to reflect your new-found understanding, and thus be more confident in your stance!

Argument

Taking a stance entails constructing an **argument** that will convince the reader or listener. As you do this, you must draw together support for your position, tying it into your own carefully constructed line of reasoning. This necessitates using information, ideas, arguments and evidence from the literature. As you are using these things to support your account or argument, it is very important that they are clearly and accurately explained.

You will need to demonstrate that you have approached your sources critically: that you have analysed, interpreted and evaluated the validity and credibility of the facts, ideas and opinions that you encounter; that you have carefully examined the reasoning behind claims, and the explanations, evidence and examples put forward in support of them.

Objectivity

It is important to demonstrate **objectivity** in your evaluation of the work of others. This involves being clear that your opinions have been formed on the basis of fact and evidence, rather than just personal feeling. You must show that you are not unduly biased in favour of a particular viewpoint or interpretation and that you are not being selective about the evidence you consider. You need to convey what you believe and provide justification for it. One way of doing this is to reference clearly, as this allows you to be transparent about what is influencing your opinion.

CROSS
REFERENCE

*Academic
Writing and
Referencing*,
Chapter 2,
Coherence
in texts and
arguments

Persuasiveness

The aim of much academic writing is to persuade the reader through the quality of your argument. You will also help persuade the reader if there is a 'persuasive structure' to your argument. For example, laying the groundwork before you make a claim will make the claim stronger, because the reader or listener can see the basis for your argument; likewise, maintaining a strong thread of argument throughout your text will make your argument more coherent and therefore more convincing. Also, a calm, objective style is more convincing than an impassioned appeal, as it shows confidence in the ability of the facts to speak for themselves.

Top tips

Acknowledge complexity

Taking a stance is not the same as being stubborn! Most academic topics are complex, with no easy answers. Therefore, your stance should be nuanced. Analysing issues from multiple perspectives, and acknowledging strengths, weaknesses and grey areas will strengthen, not weaken your argument, as you are protecting it from attack for being too simplistic. In fact, it may well be that you find, after reviewing all the evidence, that there is not enough convincing support for one particular viewpoint and that further research is needed; many systematic literature reviews in reputable journals reach this very conclusion!

Demonstrating criticality in your clinical practice

Critical thinking is a crucial part of clinical practice, and an integral feature of the Nursing and Midwifery Council's Code (2015).

Task

1) Look at the extracts from the Code below. With reference to the guidance provided in this chapter, identify the language which highlights the clear need for a critical approach:

   1.3 Avoid making assumptions and recognise diversity and individual choice.

   6.1 Make sure that any information or advice given is evidence-based.

   8.4 Work with colleagues to evaluate the quality of your work and that of your team.

   9.2 Gather and reflect on feedback from a variety of sources, using it to improve practice and performance.

   13.1 Accurately assess signs of normal or worsening physical health in the person receiving care.

   19.2 Take account of current evidence, knowledge and developments in reducing mistakes and the effect of them.

   20.6 Stay objective and have clear professional boundaries at all times with people in your care (including those who have been in your care in the past) and their families and carers.

2) Think of ways in which you could successfully meet these aspects of the Code both in theory (what you learn in the classroom) and in practice (what you learn while on placement).

Case studies

- Explain the critical thinking process that the practitioners in the situations below would need to go through. You may wish to refer back to Figure 4.1 and reflect on the qualities they would need to demonstrate.

   1) A mental health service user asks his community mental health nurse why he needs to take anti-psychotic medication when it makes him gain weight and feel tired.

   2) A nursing ward manager feels she is short-staffed and asks the hospital management for two additional registered nurses. They agree to provide more staff but, because of cost constraints, they only agree to two nursing assistants. The ward manager claims this is not acceptable as it will have a detrimental effect on patient safety. The hospital management agree to look at their decision again, but ask the ward manager for evidence that patients will be at greater risk if nursing assistants rather than registered nurses are provided.

   3) The parent of a young person with a learning disability, who also has diabetes, asks a diabetes nurse to speak to the young person directly about their treatment rather than to them as a parent.

Summary

This chapter has introduced the concept of criticality and examined its role in academic life and clinical practice. It has suggested ways of approaching learning and sources in a critical way. It has provided strategies for critical reading and provided a framework for approaching academic journal articles. It has identified strategies for presenting your ideas critically in assessments.

References

Beireiter, C and Scardamalia, M (1987) *The Psychology of Written Composition*. Hillsdale, NJ: Lawrence Erlbaum Associates.

Borton, T (1970) *Reach, Touch and Teach: Student Concerns and Process Education*. London: Hutchinson.

Chambers 21st Century Dictionary (1999) Edinburgh: Chambers Harrap Publishers Ltd.

Merriam-Webster Dictionary [online]. Available at: www.merriam-webster.com (accessed 16 March 2017).

NMC (Nursing and Midwifery Council) (2015) *The Code: Professional Standards of Practice and Behaviour for Nurses and Midwives* [online]. Available at: www.nmc.org.uk/globalassets/sitedocuments/nmc-publications/nmc-code.pdf (accessed 16 March 2017).

Oxford Living Dictionaries: English [online]. Available at: https://en.oxforddictionaries.com/ (accessed 16 March 2017).

Pryjmachuk, S, Graham, T, Haddad, M and Tylee, A (2011) School Nurses' Perspectives on Managing Mental Health Problems in Children and Young People. *Journal of Clinical Nursing*, 21: 850–9 [online]. Available at: www.ncbi.nlm.nih.gov/pubmed/21883575 (accessed 16 March 2017).

Sax, H, Allegranzi, B, Uçkay, I, Larson, E, Boyce, J and Pittet, D (2007) 'My Five Moments for Hand Hygiene': A User-centred Design Approach to Understand, Train, Monitor and Report Hand Hygiene. *Journal of Hospital Infection*, 67: 9–21 [online]. Available at: https://eportal.mountsinai.ca/Microbiology//coreEducModules/hand-hygiene-aug-2007.pdf (accessed 16 March 2017).

Chapter 5
Academic resources:
technology and the library

Learning outcomes

After reading this chapter you will:

- have gained an understanding of technology and the scope of the technological resources available to you at university;
- be able to access a range of computer hardware and software with confidence;
- appreciate the value and the limitations of the internet;
- understand the standards and regulations which govern the use of technology in universities;
- be prepared to make effective use of the university library;
- be able to carry out a basic literature search.

The aim of this chapter is to provide you with knowledge and strategies which will enable you to make full use of the resources available to you at university. It will help you understand how technology and the university library can help you develop your research and communication skills, and generally enhance your nursing studies.

For a discussion of the role of e-learning methods and tools such as blended learning and Virtual Learning Environments (VLEs), see Chapter 1.

CROSS
REFERENCE

Chapter 1,
Studying
nursing
in higher
education

Understanding technology and developing good computer skills

In its strictest sense, 'technology' is the application of science to practical, real-world situations; it is *applied* science. Since learning is inextricably linked to *information*, educators are primarily concerned with **information technology (IT)**, or **information and communication technology (ICT)**.

It is useful to divide technology into two components: **hardware** and **software**.

Hardware

Hardware is the physical equipment that you can touch. It includes:

- computers, including laptops and tablets;
- phones, including landlines, mobiles and smartphones;
- media recorders such as cameras and camcorders;
- media players such as MP3, CD and DVD players;
- portable storage devices known as pen drives, USB memory sticks etc;
- gaming consoles such as Wii, Nintendo DS, Xbox and PlayStation.

Reflection

1) How might the different types of hardware be of use to you in your university studies and in nursing practice?
2) What issues or problems may accompany their use?

Discussion of hardware uses at university

Compare your ideas from the reflection with those in Table 5.1.

Table 5.1: Types of hardware

HARDWARE	SOME USES	SOME ISSUES AND PROBLEMS
Computers	Main research and communication tool (discussed in detail later in the next section); laptops and tablets useful for note-taking in lectures	Information on the internet must be treated with caution; overuse may lead to conditions such as repetitive strain injury (RSI)
Phones	Contacting students and lecturers; photographing the screen during lectures	Need to be aware of 'mobile phone etiquette' such as making sure phones are silenced in lectures (not turned off – there may be legitimate use of a phone in a lecture, accessing a dictionary for example); may need permission for some photos
Media recorders and players	Recording and playing back recorded material such as lectures and interviews	Make sure you have permission to record things
Portable storage devices	Backing up files and moving files between devices	Small pen drives are easy to misplace – many are left behind in university computer drives; security issues – computer viruses are easily transferred with these
Gaming consoles	Some have suggested educational uses, but they are perhaps mostly useful for helping some people to switch off and relax	Make sure they don't distract you from study or disrupt your sleep patterns

Computers in particular are now an essential part of studying. They are invaluable tools for word processing assignments, creating presentation slides, searching for information, carrying out statistical analysis, and communicating with others.

Most universities are extremely well resourced when it comes to computers, with 'clusters' of computers set up throughout their campuses. Almost all the computers in a university are 'networked' (joined to one another), and to access them you will need a **username** and **password**. Details of how to obtain these will be provided when you commence your programme of study.

Software

Software is what runs on the hardware to enable you to process the information you are interested in. With the advent of smartphones, tablets and other portable devices, software has come to be known as **apps** (from 'software applications').

It will benefit your studies if you can develop an understanding of what software is available, and how you can access and use it.

Office suites

Office suites are integrated software packages containing a number of different programs that are useful in an office, business or educational environment. As a minimum, they include word processing, presentation and spreadsheet software, but many other components are available to suit individual needs. The most well-known office suites are **Microsoft Office** and **OpenOffice**. Microsoft Office is a commercial program which you normally have to pay for, but free access is almost always provided by universities for registered students. OpenOffice is 'open source', meaning that it is freely available; it is also compatible with Microsoft Office, which means users can work across systems easily. The software in these suites resides on individual computers or, in large organisations such as universities, on a server which manages access to centralised resources and services in the network. **Google Docs** and Apple's **iWork** are slightly different types of office suite in that their software sits in the cloud on the internet rather than on a computer or server; cloud technology is further discussed later in the chapter.

As a university student, you will probably receive a free account such as **Office 365** for the duration of your studies. This will give you access to software, including email.

The components of an office suite that are likely to be most useful to you in your studies are:

- word processing software;
- presentation software;
- spreadsheet software;
- communication software.

You may also use software to help you analyse data or to help you reference, as discussed later in the chapter.

CROSS REFERENCE

Advanced skills, Advanced software

Word processing

Word processing packages turn your computer into a sophisticated typewriter. The most well known is **Microsoft Word**. Word processing offers huge advantages over hand-writing and old-fashioned typewriting: documents can be easily edited; many different fonts are available; pictures and diagrams can be easily inserted into documents; links to other documents can be included via **hyperlinks** (highlighted words or images which you can click on); tools are available to help you format documents professionally.

Top tips

Formatting

Try not to think of formatting as something merely 'cosmetic', there just to make the page look nice. Clear presentation will make your work instantly more professional. What's more, clear and consistent formatting will contribute to the **coherence** of the text. Carefully distinguished headings and sub-headings, together with clearly set out paragraphs and sections, will help the reader move smoothly through the text. A well-chosen font (Times New Roman or Arial) and font size (usually 12pt) will also positively affect the reader's experience, as will the use of 1.5 or double line spacing. Last but not least, don't forget page numbers. (Pity the poor lecturer shuffling papers on the train to work!)

CROSS REFERENCE

Academic Writing and Referencing, Chapter 5, Preparing your work for submission

Word processing software has many user-friendly tools, available on the tool bar as icons or in drop-down menus. These include 'cut' and 'paste', which allows you to move text around easily, and the 'undo' command, which allows you to reverse one or several actions.

Top tips

Keyboard shortcuts

If you use the **Microsoft Windows** operating system, as the majority of students do, there are a number of keyboard shortcuts which will save you time and effort (ctrl = control, the key in the bottom left-hand corner of your keyboard):

ctrl O = open file

ctrl S = save file

ctrl P = print file

ctrl A = select all the text in a document

ctrl C = copy selected text or item

ctrl X = cut selected text or item

ctrl V = paste selected text or item

ctrl Z = undo previous action

ctrl B = make selected text **bold**

ctrl I = make selected text *italic*

ctrl U = <u>underline</u> selected text

Apple Mac shortcuts can be found here:
https://support.apple.com/en-gb/HT201236

Presentations

The most well-known presentation software is **Microsoft PowerPoint**, but **Prezi** is also increasingly popular. With both of these, a series of slides is created which form the basis of a presentation, and these can be formatted by choosing a suitable slide design, font etc. There is also the possibility of creating or uploading pictures, diagrams etc. These slides can be very simple, or layers of complexity can be added through the use of the **transition** (movement between slides) and **animation** (movement within slides) tools. With PowerPoint, you move through the slides chronologically during your presentation; with Prezi, you pan between topics, zooming in on detail or zooming out to reveal the wider context.

It is important to make your slides readable for everyone in the audience, and to make your presentation as inclusive as possible. This entails making provision, where you can, for audience members who may have a particular condition, such as visual impairment, or a specific learning difficulty, such as dyslexia.

Top tips

Presentation slides

- Choose a font size that's visible at the back of the room (24pt is usually the lower limit, but it depends on other factors – room, size of screen etc).
- Be wary of using **bold**, *italics*, <u>underlining</u> or CAPITALISATION to convey subtleties of meaning, as these are hard to read on screen, particularly for anyone who is dyslexic.
- Don't make the slides too cluttered with text or images.
- Make sure diagrams and labels are clearly visible.
- Avoid decorative background images that may obscure the text.
- Make sure there is a clear colour contrast between background and text (and remember that just because it's clear on your computer at home, it doesn't mean it necessarily will be on a classroom screen with different resolution and lighting conditions – always check *in situ*).
- Avoid using red and green together, as people who have a colour vision deficiency (the formal name for 'colour blindness') cannot distinguish between them.
- Moving images or flashing effects can be distracting or even irritating – they may also be dangerous for people with epilepsy or light-sensitivity.

CROSS
REFERENCE

*Communication
Skills*, Chapter
1, Academic
presentations
and public
speaking

- If you use the animation **appear** function, plan how to synchronise the appearance of each bullet point with a segment of your speech – there's no point using the appear function if you introduce all the bullet points at once.

See *Communication Skills* for more tips on creating and delivering presentations.

Top tips

Presentation technology: less is more?

There is no doubt that PowerPoint and Prezi are very visual tools with an effective 'story telling' function which can genuinely help you convey information and ideas. What's more, clever use of diagrams, transitions and animations can truly enhance your presentation: for example, an audience could be guided through the stages of a biological process such as *digestion* with a diagram that is gradually added to using the 'appear' function. The diagram below could be presented and explained in three separate stages (1; +2; +3), allowing the audience to process one piece of information before moving on to the next:

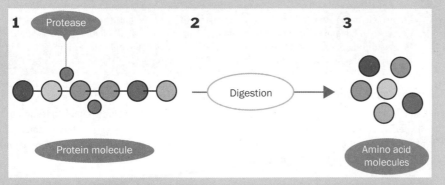

Figure 5.1: The digestion of proteins (adapted from BBC Bitesize)

However, any 'special effects' should be integral to the main aim of the presentation, which should always be to convey information and ideas in the clearest possible way to the audience. Too many 'showy' animations can be a distraction.

Ultimately, presentation software is an **organisational tool**, and complex ideas almost always benefit from a **simple organisational structure** and **clear and consistent formatting**.

Spreadsheets

Spreadsheet software is extremely useful for work which requires mathematical or financial calculations. The most well known is **Microsoft Excel**. While you won't use spreadsheet software as much as word processing and presentation software in your studies, spreadsheets do have uses in nursing and healthcare. For example: they are used by ward managers to receive and analyse financial information; they might be used to organise off-duty rosters; and they are often used to record specific data about patients in research studies.

Top tips

Working smart

As a student, it won't be long before you have created a number of different files, be they word processing documents, presentations or spreadsheets, and it is extremely important that you know where these are and that you don't somehow lose or inadvertently delete them.

1) Always make sure you **save**, and ideally, **back up** your work. There are many ways to save work, including:
   - your university's networked drive;
   - a USB memory stick;
   - cloud services such as **Dropbox**, **Google Docs**, **Apple iCloud** and **OneDrive**.

   The most secure of these is your university's networked drive, as it can only be accessed using your university login and password, and, crucially, it is backed up frequently by the university, so it is extremely unlikely that you will lose your work. In addition, as it is networked, you can access this drive anywhere in the world as long as you have an internet connection. For these reasons, this is the best way to save your work, particularly anything which is important.

   You may also choose to use USB memory sticks and cloud services, but be aware of the limitations of these. As mentioned earlier, USB sticks are easy to lose and can transmit viruses. Cloud services may not necessarily be backed up and, more importantly, they may not meet UK or university data protection requirements.

2) Make sure you organise your work in a systematic way. It is a good idea to create folders to save your work according to topic; otherwise, your drive will soon become unwieldy and untidy. Experiment with organisational systems until you find something that works for you. Choose file names which are as short and simple as possible, but which easily identify the content of a file and distinguish it from others. Some people add the date to the file name (eg healthpromotionessay-02feb16.doc), which is useful if you want to keep and go back to an earlier version of your work – to restore something you deleted, for example.

Communication software

You can use computers to communicate in a variety of ways. These include: email, messaging and **Skype/FaceTime**, all of which require an internet connection. There is a variety of email software, including the cloud-based **Microsoft Outlook**, which is included in Office 365, and web-based email services such as Google's **Gmail**.

Top tips

Your university email address

Your university will provide you with a university email, and even though you may well have one or more other email accounts, you should always use your university email to communicate with staff and other students and for all university business. As you will no doubt be aware, there is a huge amount of junk email, or 'spam' about. With a view to managing spam, universities have filtering systems, and this may affect emails from web-based accounts, especially if the address contains dubious words! You should check your university account regularly as this is how the university will contact you. This is also where VLE updates and announcements will automatically be sent.

Messaging services can be synchronous or asynchronous: synchronous means that all the participants in the 'chat' can communicate at the same time; asynchronous means that each piece of text has to be posted somewhere, ie to a relevant discussion board or forum, and participants have to wait for responses.

The most well-known synchronous service is instant messaging – you may be familiar with examples such as **WhatsApp**. Instant messaging 'chat' can be restricted to those you know or invite, or it can take place with lesser-known acquaintances or even strangers in what are known as 'chat rooms'. This software is especially useful for communicating over long distances, and it now often includes audio and video functions.

Asynchronous messaging is commonly conducted in universities through **discussion boards**, which are usually part of your VLE. Unlike with synchronous messaging, the messages you post on discussion boards will usually be archived, so there will be a permanent record. It is therefore worth taking a little longer to consider the tone and content of your posts.

Skype provides all the basics of instant messaging plus phone use. Some members of staff at university may choose to communicate with you using Skype, especially if they are working away from the university for some reason.

CROSS
REFERENCE

*Communication
Skills*, Chapter
4, Networking

Advanced skills

Advanced software

Your university library will probably provide information and training on a number of more specialised software applications.

1) Third-year undergraduates and postgraduates will probably need technical help in analysing their data. Those undertaking **quantitative** research (research including 'quantities', ie numbers) may need to make use of specialised **statistical software**. The most well-known of these are **SPSS** and **Stata**. Those undertaking **qualitative** research (research concerned with 'qualities', ie experiences, feelings, perceptions etc) might use software like **Nvivo** to help them manage and analyse their data.

2) As you begin to write longer, fully-referenced essays and dissertations, you may choose to employ referencing management software such as **Endnote**, **Mendeley**, **Zotero** and **Papyrus**.

CROSS
REFERENCE

*Academic
Writing and
Referencing*,
Chapter 3,
Referring to
sources

The internet

The internet is the most powerful information and communication tool in existence, and it has transformed all our lives. You will no doubt be aware of both its potential and its challenges in modern society.

Reflection

Pros and cons of the internet

- Consider some of the positive and negative aspects of the internet in each of the following areas (which are discussed in more detail in the rest of this section):

    1) information retrieval, in particular on topics related to nursing and health issues;

    2) storing data and files online;

    3) social media;

    4) security.

The internet is a vast global collection of computers. The computers in your university will be connected to the internet and you will probably have a **broadband** connection at home. The most important part of the internet is the **World Wide Web**, or 'the **Web**', containing text, images, videos etc, and usually **hypertext** (links to other web pages). Web pages have a **URL** (Uniform Resource Locator) address beginning with 'www.'. For example, the URL of the Nursing and Midwifery Council is www.nmc.org.uk. Different websites have different 'domain names' (at the end of the address) depending on their status, eg:

- .com = company;
- .org.uk = UK charities;
- .gov.uk = official UK government sites;
- .ac.uk = UK universities.

Below are some websites you may find useful during your nursing studies:

Table 5.2: Useful nursing study websites

GENERAL WEBSITES	
The Student Room	www.thestudentroom.co.uk
StudentMidwife.net	www.studentmidwife.net

PROFESSIONAL BODIES AND HEALTH UNIONS	
Royal College of Nursing	www.rcn.org.uk
Royal College of Midwives	www.rcm.org.uk
Community Practitioners and Health Visitors Association	www.unitetheunion.org/cphva
Mental Health Nurses Association	www.unitetheunion.org/mhna
Unison (public services union)	www.unison.org.uk

STATUTORY AND REGULATORY WEBSITES	
Department of Health	www.gov.uk/government/organisations/department-of-health
Department of Health Social Care sub-site	www.gov.uk/government/topics/social-care
Nursing & Midwifery Council	www.nmc.org.uk
National Institute for Health and Care Excellence (NICE)	www.nice.org.uk
Health & Care Professions Council (regulates social workers, psychologists, physiotherapists, etc)	www.hcpc-uk.org
Social Care Institute for Excellence	www.scie.org.uk
Care Quality Commission	www.cqc.org.uk

PUBLICATIONS	
Nursing Standard online	www.nursing-standard.co.uk
Nursing Times online	www.nursingtimes.co.uk
Community Care online	www.communitycare.co.uk
British Journal of Nursing	www.magonlinelibrary.com/journal/bjon
Nursing in Practice	www.nursinginpractice.com
International Journal of Nursing Studies	www.journalofnursingstudies.com
Midwifery	www.midwiferyjournal.com
British Journal of Midwifery	www.magonlinelibrary.com/journal/bjom

To view web pages such as those listed in Table 5.2, you need a **web browser**, the most well known of which are Microsoft's **Internet Explorer**, Google's **Chrome**, Apple's **Safari** and The Mozilla Foundation's **Firefox**. VLEs sometimes have compatibility issues with certain browsers; you will need to check with your university's IT department.

The cloud

The 'cloud' has been a buzzword in computing for a number of years. Cloud computing means that the software you use – word processing, statistical analysis etc – sits in the cloud on the internet rather than being on your actual computer or server. It is therefore accessed using an internet connection and a browser. It is a very practical and convenient tool which can help you manage your work. However, it may not be as secure as your university networked drive, so make sure anything important is also saved on the latter.

Social media

Social media includes social networking sites such as **Facebook**, **Twitter**, **Instagram** and **YouTube**. It also includes **blogs** and **wikis**. A blog is a public online diary. Well-known blog sites include **WordPress.com** and Google's **Blogger**. A wiki is an online platform that enables people to work collaboratively on documents. (The most well-known collaborative document is **Wikipedia**.) Sites where you can find software to build wikis include **PB Works**, **PmWiki**, **TWiki** and **MediaWiki**. Social media is quite a contentious area with many concerns over online behaviour and security, some of which will be discussed in the next section.

Online behaviour and security

When using communication software and the internet, it is necessary to demonstrate a degree of caution. There are two big safety threats when you are online: the first is to the actual computer you are using; the second is to yourself.

Computer security

The big threat to computers, especially those connected to the internet, is 'malware', ie malicious software. The most common type of malware is the computer virus, which can destroy data and corrupt your system; other types include 'spyware', software that is designed to steal personal information such as the sites you visit or even your passwords. To protect against threats to the computer you are using, you need to ensure that your computer's operating system is up to date and that you have anti-virus and anti-spyware software installed. Universities often make anti-virus packages such as **Sophos** and **McAfee** freely available to to their registered students.

Personal security

The online threat to you personally may be an attempt to steal your identity, or it may be an actual threat to your safety from another person. But the risk can also be to your reputation. Damage to your reputation or image can have far-reaching consequences: poor behaviour, an unguarded comment or an embarrassing photograph could be seen by a prospective employer, for example. The code of good manners and behaviour online is known as **netiquette** (a portmanteau of 'etiquette' – good manners in social interaction – and 'internet'). Netiquette is part of the professional behaviour that is expected of students and those working in care professions like nursing. The rules of netiquette are aimed to protect you and others from harm and embarrassment. They require you to behave with politeness and to avoid the following.

- Inappropriate emails. You are in a professional relationship with staff, and the emails you write to them should not contain things you might send to friends, such as slang or kisses.

- 'Empty' emails, with just an attachment but no information. All emails to staff should contain:
  - a clear subject heading, eg 'Group presentation slides';
  - a polite salutation with the correct name, eg 'Dear Dr Gonzalez';
  - a clear, concise message, eg 'Please find attached …';
  - a polite sign-off, eg 'Regards, Peter'.
- Lack of patience in relation to responses to emails. Academic staff are very busy so don't expect an immediate response; it isn't unreasonable to expect a response within 48 hours, but remember, some staff are part time and may not look at their emails every day.

CROSS
REFERENCE

*Communication
Skills,*
Chapter 6,
Networking

- Forwarding dubious emails: this includes chain emails or likely hoaxes.
- Posting personal information on discussion boards. This includes information about yourself, other students and your lecturers.
- Adopting an inappropriate tone or language on discussion boards. This includes being careful about upper-case words and exclamation marks, which can seem a bit angry in a discussion context.

Note that the NMC Code (2015) requires that nurses and midwives use all forms of spoken, written and digital communication, including social media and social networking sites, responsibly.

The university library

The focal point for your university's study resources will be the library. The importance of the university library cannot be overestimated: it is the hub of all scholarly institutions. Academic libraries provide access to specialist textbooks and journals that you will not find in your local library. Moreover, modern academic libraries are now so much more than collections of books housed under the library roof (though this is still an important part of what they do); they are also the source of huge amounts of information and advice which can help you in all aspects of your learning and development. Advances in technology mean that many modern library services are electronic or online, creating a 'virtual library'. You will be able to access many materials and services without actually having to walk into the university library building at all.

Your university library will almost certainly have a specific web page for nursing students, and may well have a specialist nursing library. As well as the university library, you will also have access to hospital libraries, which have a wealth of material relevant to healthcare professionals.

University libraries also provide many other services such as:

- inter-library loans;
- photocopying, scanning and printing services;
- librarians – the most useful resource in the library!

Don't be afraid to ask librarians for help – that is why they are there! They have huge amounts of expertise, often specialising in particular subjects. They are perhaps better regarded as 'information specialists'. Check your library website to see which librarian specialises in nursing.

CROSS
REFERENCE

*Academic
Writing and
Referencing,*
Chapter 3,
Referring to
sources

Knowing what's out there

Be aware of the different resources available to you in the library and its online virtual counterpart, including the following.

- **Textbooks**: these can be either *standard* textbooks, ie written by one author or a small number of co-authors working together on the text, or *edited* textbooks, ie where different authors (sometimes including the editor/editors) write each chapter separately, and the editor's job is to give the book overall consistency. This distinction is important when it comes to referencing. Many textbooks will be available as ebooks.

- **Academic journals and periodicals**: these are published at regular intervals and reflect advances in a particular area represented by the title itself. Journals are the more academic of the two: they are peer reviewed, ie the articles in them have been subject to a review by an expert panel of referees. With periodicals, it tends to be the editor who decides what is published. In nursing, important journals include:

  - *Journal of Advanced Nursing*;
  - *Journal of Clinical Nursing*;
  - *International Journal of Nursing Studies*;
  - *Journal of Psychiatric and Mental Health Nursing*;
  - *Midwifery*.

  Periodicals include:

  - *Nursing Times*;
  - *Nursing Standard*;
  - *Community Care*.

  There is a hierarchy of journals and periodicals: some carry more weight than others. This weight is measured in academia by something called an **impact factor** (Garfield, 2006). As you progress through your academic studies, you will be expected to be more dependent on these weightier journals. Most of these journals and periodicals are available online and you will often have free-of-charge access to them via your university library.

- **Reference material**: this includes dictionaries, encyclopaedias, directories, registers (eg the Medical Register) and official reports.
- **Bibliographies, indices and abstracts**: these are special publications which list and summarise all the articles which have been published in a given subject over a specific period of time. For example, the 1996 volume of CINAHL (Cumulative Index of Nursing and Allied Health Literature) lists all the papers published in nursing and related subjects in 1996. These are now usually in the form of online databases, which are discussed below.
- **Official reports and papers**: these could be Acts of Parliament, or reports from government, statuary bodies or voluntary organisations. A lot of these documents are now published only online, usually as a free PDF.
- **Online newspapers**.

Conducting a literature search

If you are writing an essay or giving a presentation, you will probably need to do a substantial amount of academic reading. Firstly, you must know how to find suitable reading material through a systematic search of the literature on that topic. Your literature search should start with the online **library search**. When you type in your search term, say 'MRSA', you will usually be given a list of books, articles etc related to the topic. Links will tell you where to locate the book in the library or provide links to ebooks and full-text copies of articles to download to your computer. (You should read the **abstract** of an article to check it really is of use before you print it out: this will save you time and money!). Particularly as you progress in your studies, you will need to consult **databases** such as **CINAHL** for a more comprehensive search. Other databases include **Maternity and Infant care, MEDLINE, EMBASE** and **PsycINFO**. In order to access these databases, you need an **interface** such as **OVID, EBSCO, ProQuest** and **PubMed**. There will be links to these interfaces, and information about the databases they provide access to, on your university library website. You can also consult your lecturers and the librarians for advice.

Identifying key search terms

Identifying key words related to your assignment will help point you in the right direction. This can involve **lateral thinking**, but this is something you're probably already used to from your own Google searches. For example, if you are looking for a flight from London to New York, you might try some of the following (in combination perhaps) to drive your search:

flights, low-cost flights,
Heathrow, Gatwick, JFK, British Airways,
Newark, American Airlines, United Airlines

Figure 5.2: Flight search terms

Task

Which key words might you try when researching the following topics?
1) behavioural interventions in schizophrenia
2) dependence and independence in older people

Refining your search

A general online library search on a common topic will generally present you with an overwhelming amount of material, so you will need to refine your search. The best way to do this is to use the **advanced search** options provided on the university library website or database interface to limit your search in some way. This could mean refining your search by date or author, for example. A particularly useful advanced search option is to combine one search term with another, eg 'MRSA' and 'surgery'.

Widening your search

Sometimes your search might not produce many results. In this case, you should try to be more creative with your searches.

- Use synonyms. For example, if the topic is 'children's views on diabetes nurses', synonyms for 'child' might be 'young person' or 'adolescent', and 'perceptions', 'experiences' or 'satisfaction' could be substituted for 'views'.

- Use truncation or wildcards. Truncation allows you to search for words with a common stem. The symbol for truncation varies across systems but it is often an asterisk (*). So the search 'nurs*' will find 'nurse', 'nurses', 'nursing' and 'nursed'. A wildcard (again, often an asterisk) can represent any character, so 'wom*n' would find 'woman' and 'women'.

- As you read, make a note of any relevant or interesting references which may enrich your search. (Always make a note of the full reference.)

Top tips

Visit the library!

With all the online tools and materials available, some students find they rarely visit the actual library. However, it can be a great place to study without distractions. Moreover, actually visiting the shelves where you know there are books on your topic, and spending some time browsing the surrounding books can be an interesting way of exploring a topic. Sometimes in this virtual world, it can be nice to feel a book in your hand!

Google and Wikipedia

Google and Wikipedia are useful resources in everyday life but they have serious limitations in academic life. Broadly speaking, the quality of the results generated by Google is not controlled. This contrasts with academic databases like CINAHL, which only contain *academic* material.

Reflection

Search for 'red wine' and 'heart disease' on Google and CINAHL and compare the results.

There are stronger arguments in favour of using **Google Scholar**, which does have a higher degree of quality control compared to a normal Google search. However, there are still downsides, so you should use it with caution.

- It does not have the sophisticated filters of interfaces like OVID.
- Companies can pay Google or manipulate searches so that they feature at the top of a Google search.
- You don't often get easy access to the full article: you may be asked to pay or you may need to get to it via an alternative route using the university website, which is more time consuming than if you'd gone there in the first place!

Wikipedia is a general encyclopaedia, and thus, like all encyclopaedias, it is usually not specialised enough for most academic study. Furthermore, it is written by whosoever feels inclined to contribute, which means that the expertise of writer cannot be guaranteed. Also, there are no peer reviewers to call the writer to account. Finally, Wikipedia is rather strange in that it generates its own references (in hyperlinks throughout the entries), a practice that would be frowned upon in academic circles.

Summary

This chapter has explored how technological and university library resources can support your university studies, particularly in terms of research and communication. It has discussed the potentially positive impact of computer technology and the internet, as well as the challenges which they present. Judicious use of technology and the university library, in both its physical and virtual forms, will help you function successfully as a student in the modern world.

References

BBC Bitesize. *Digestive System* [online]. Available at: www.bbc.co.uk/education/guides/z9pv34j/revision/2 (accessed 16 March 2017).

Garfield, E (2006) The History and Meaning of the Journal Impact Factor. *JAMA*, 295(1): 90–3 [online]. Available at: http://garfield.library.upenn.edu/papers/jamajif2006.pdf (accessed 16 March 2017).

NMC (Nursing and Midwifery Council) (2015) *The Code: Professional Standards of Practice and Behaviour for Nurses and Midwives* [online]. Available at: www.nmc.org.uk/globalassets/sitedocuments/nmc-publications/nmc-code.pdf (accessed 16 March 2017).

Chapter 6
Assessment

Learning outcomes

After reading this chapter you will:

- have gained an overview of assessment in HE;
- be better equipped to approach assessment and deal with stress and anxiety caused by it;
- have gained an understanding of the different types of assessment common in universities and nursing degrees;
- be aware of the importance of feedback in your academic development;
- be more able to interpret feedback from tutors.

Assessment is an integral part of student life. Different people respond in different ways to assessment, but most people find it challenging. It is very important to be well informed on this aspect of your studies, and to develop strategies to enable you to perform to the very best of your ability in essays, exams, presentations, and practical and clinical assessments. You also need to manage the stress and anxiety associated with assessment. This chapter will examine the aims of assessment and explain how it is carried out in HE. It will help you to approach assessment tasks in a positive way, and to understand the crucial role that feedback from your tutors plays in your academic development.

Reflection

1) What kind of assessment have you done in the past?
2) How did you feel about it?
3) Did you feel it was a fair test of your knowledge and abilities?

Assessment in higher education

As a student nurse, you will be assessed through coursework, exams and tests of your clinical (practice) abilities. These provide **evidence** of your knowledge and understanding of the subject matter of your degree programme, and of your ability to apply it to clinical practice. Assessments in HE have different purposes, depending on the stage you are at in your studies, as illustrated in Table 6.1.

Table 6.1: Assessment types (adapted from University of Manchester School of Nursing, Midwifery and Social Work, 2014)

TYPE OF ASSESSMENT	PURPOSE	IN OTHER WORDS ...
Diagnostic	To determine your current level of knowledge and skills	What do I know?
Formative	To give you a chance to practise something, or to start something and receive feedback before continuing	How am I doing?
Summative	To sum up/establish what you have learned and/or can do and assign a mark/grade based on that performance	How did I do?

Summative assessment of a module is directly related to the **learning outcomes** of the course module – what you should be able to *understand* or *do*.

If you are an international student, you will normally be required to provide evidence of your English language proficiency in order to be accepted onto a university course. This is normally through a particular type of summative test, usually the International English Language Testing System (IELTS) or the Test of English as a Foreign Language (TOEFL).

Submission and marking of assessments

Currently, most universities require students to submit written assessments on their VLE using plagiarism-detection software such as **Turnitin**, which compares your writing with published sources and other submitted essays to ensure it is all your own work. You may also be asked to submit other items, such as presentation slides.

There are many safeguards in place to ensure that the assessment procedure is fair and transparent.

- Submission procedures are usually designed to make all work anonymous.
- A proportion of assignments are moderated (marked by the main assessor and a second marker) for consistency.
- An external examiner (an academic from another university) reviews the assessments, the assessment process and the marks to make sure that everything is fair and consistent.

Most assessed work is marked using **descriptors** which specify the **criteria** that you need to meet in order to achieve a particular mark. These will be closely aligned to the **learning outcomes** of the module and may well be referred to in lectures, seminars etc.

An effective approach to assessment

In order to do well in assessments, it is necessary to approach them in a systematic way.

Inform yourself

It is very important to start an assessment by informing yourself. This means reading the **assessment guidelines** and familiarising yourself with the marking descriptors. It may also involve discussing any queries you have regarding the assessment with your lecturer. This essential familiarisation process is sometimes overlooked: it is not unknown for students to glance at an essay title and go off and write something vaguely connected which they rather fancy writing but which, unfortunately, doesn't address the task! Such an essay may be interesting, and even well written, but if it does not answer the question or address the task, follow the guidelines, or meet the relevant marking criteria, it will not get a high mark. Lecturers do not enjoy giving low marks, but they can only give high marks if the precise criteria in the descriptors are met.

Plan and manage your time

Give yourself a timetable for completing course assignments and stick to it as closely as possible. This timetable should cover:

- familiarising yourself with the assessment guidelines and marking criteria;
- brainstorming your current knowledge of the topic;
- reviewing lecture notes;
- conducting a literature search;
- reading;
- writing an essay/report/presentation plan or outline (which can be revisited and refined);
- writing a first draft of an essay/report or creating draft slides for a presentation;

CROSS REFERENCE

Chapter 1, Studying nursing in higher education, Courses and credits

- editing and redrafting written work or presentation slides;
- formatting your work;
- proofreading your work;
- practising presentations;
- double-checking the assessment guidelines and marking criteria to make sure you have met all the requirements.

An important aspect of assessment is **time management**. You should make sure you start assignments in good time. Begin by reading the guidelines and marking criteria straight away, so that you have time to make an appointment with a lecturer if you need to raise any queries. It is also important to start planning and writing as soon as possible. You may sometimes be able to submit a plan or first draft to your lecturer; be sure to use the feedback from this to help you improve your assignment.

Planning gives you control and a sense of progress, and breaking down a large task into smaller manageable chunks can help you avoid stress and anxiety.

Written assessments

Written assessments test both your understanding of the topic and your academic writing skills. Your nursing assessments may include:

- reports;
- portfolios, which might include written reflections and personal journals or logs;
- essays;
- dissertations.

Reports

Reports require you to present information accurately, usually following a very precise structure. For example, you might be asked to write a report on an individual (anonymised or hypothetical) patient with headings such as:

- background;
- principal presenting problem;
- nursing assessment;
- care plan;
- review period.

CROSS REFERENCE

Chapter 3, Joining your academic and professional community, Reflective practice

Portfolios

These are a collection of materials which provide evidence of your performance in a number of areas. You might be assessed on the individual items (eg written reflections) and/or the overall coherence of the portfolio. Portfolio assessments often include an assessment on your capacity to demonstrate self-awareness and reflection.

Essays

An essay is a response to a question or statement which requires you to explore a particular topic in detail. This usually involves the development of an argument and the expression of an independent viewpoint, emerging from your engagement with critical debate in the literature. In nursing, you may be asked to write a reflective essay, in which you analyse your experiences and their impact on your development. Essays vary in form and length, but they usually have the following in common:

- a precise **purpose**, detailed in the essay question or the prescriptions of the essay title;

- a target **reader** – lecturers may ask you to imagine addressing an educated non-expert or a first-year undergraduate (to make sure that you explicitly demonstrate your understanding and do not just expect the reader to read between the lines);
- a particular **structure**, usually indicated by **headings** and **sub-headings**;
- a formal, objective **academic writing style**;
- **references** to the literature on the topic, presented according to standard referencing conventions: in nursing, the **Harvard** (name–date) system tends to be used.

Dissertations

At the end of your course, you will most likely be required to write a long evidence-based or research-focused essay usually between 10,000 and 20,000 words. This is known as a **dissertation**. For many students, this is the first time that they have attempted such an extended piece of work, and it can be quite a daunting prospect. You might be able to find copies of past dissertations in your university library or by asking your lecturers, and looking at these will help you understand what you need to produce.

Like all the work you do at university, a dissertation must be 'original'. This does not mean that you are expected to make a major discovery in your field! It might mean, for example, that you conduct your own review of the evidence surrounding a particular nursing practice, treatment or care approach. Because of the strict ethics associated with conducting research, undergraduate nursing students tend not to do *research* dissertations, though this is an expectation of most postgraduate dissertations.

Oral assessments

Oral assessments are usually academic presentations, but you may also be assessed on seminar participation in some courses. Rarely for undergraduate students, though almost always used as part of PhD thesis assessments, the *viva voce* (usually shortened to *viva*) is a specific form of oral assessment.

Presentations test your understanding of the topic, your oral communication skills and your use of presentation software such as PowerPoint or Prezi. You may be asked to do individual or group presentations. Some presentations may be 'poster' presentations, where you talk around a poster containing an overview of your topic – these can also be done by individuals or groups. Group presentations partly test your collaborative skills; poster presentations will particularly test your ability to convey information and ideas in a concise, visually appealing form.

CROSS REFERENCE

Academic Writing and Referencing

CROSS REFERENCE

Chapter 3, Becoming a member of your academic and professional community, Advanced skills, Research reports

CROSS REFERENCE

Academic Writing and Referencing

Top tips

Public speaking: reducing stress and anxiety

Most people suffer nerves when speaking in public – the proverbial 'butterflies' in the stomach! It is actually a good sign in a way – it shows you care about what you are doing and have respect for your audience. However, there are some strategies that you can adopt to help stem the nerves a little and reduce stress and anxiety.

1) **Keep it simple**. Complex content benefits from a **simple organisational structure**, and the simpler it is, the easier it is to remember.

2) **Use an *aide-memoire***. This is usually in the form of brief notes on cards. Some people find it useful to note down 'transition' phrases such as 'I'll now move on to discuss some of the limitations of the study' to help them move between slides (often the point when you lose your train of thought). Presentation software often allows notes to be made that the presenter can see but not the audience.

3) **Practise**. Practise several times to help you remember what you want to say, improve your delivery and increase your confidence.

CROSS
REFERENCE

Chapter 5,
Academic
resources:
technology
and the library,
Presentations

4) **Check the pronunciation of key words**. Use an online dictionary with sound function (or a specialised reference work for very technical words), especially if English is not your first language. Assessors will not penalise you for having an accent (we all do!) or for the occasional mispronunciation, but they will be irritated if you keep mispronouncing a key word, or they will be unable to follow if they cannot make out which word you are trying to say. Being prepared will reduce anxiety.

5) **Don't learn by rote**. Practice does not mean learning by rote – each practice attempt should follow the same basic structure, perhaps with some repeated phrases written down as an aide-memoire, but there should also be some normal variation. It will sound unnatural if you try to recite something you have memorised, and straining to remember will make you stressed and preoccupied, preventing engagement with the audience.

6) **Don't panic**. If you lose your train of thought, pause and consult your notes or slides. Audiences are usually fairly sympathetic – they probably know how you feel!

7) **Slow down**. It's quite common for people to speak too quickly in presentations, especially if they are nervous. Make a conscious effort to slow down, pause occasionally and breathe! You will then feel more in control.

CROSS
REFERENCE

*Communi-
cation Skills*,
Chapter 1,
Academic
presentations
and public
speaking

Exams

Exams are a way of checking that you understand the core work covered on a course. Exams have many different forms and functions, but they all test your ability to recall information under strict time constraints, a very useful skill in both education and nursing practice.

Exams can be 'seen', whereby you are given the topic beforehand and can prepare your answer, or 'unseen', whereby you can be asked to answer questions about anything you have studied on a particular module. Some exams are 'open-book', which means you can consult books, articles and materials during the exam. Some exams are multiple choice, requiring you to select the right answer from the given options. Alternatively, you may be required to provide short or long written answers to questions. Examples of nursing exam questions are given below.

Example exam questions

Multiple choice
(The correct answers are indicated with an asterisk.)
1) Which of the following is not an element of the nursing process?
   a) Assessment
   b) Planning
   c) Evaluation
   d) Discussion (*)
2) Where can the adrenal glands be found?
   a) In the brain
   b) Above the kidneys (*)
   c) In the neck
   d) In the testicles (only men have them)

Short answer
1) Give some examples of what might be called 'long-term conditions' in physical and mental health.
2) What are the most common risk factors associated with pre-eclampsia?

Long answer
1) Outline what you would do as a qualified nurse to raise and/or escalate concerns you had about clinical practice.
2) Critically explore the evidence for the use of cognitive-behaviour therapy (CBT) with 'medically-unexplained' symptoms.

Top tips

Past papers

Universities provide online access to past exam papers, usually through their library websites. Looking at these as part of your revision can be an invaluable aid in helping you to understand the types of questions you may be asked. Testing your recall against these can also make you aware of gaps in your knowledge which you need to revise.

Exam technique

There are certain strategies that you can adopt during an exam which will help you perform to the best of your ability and help you manage stress and anxiety.

1) **Check the whole paper**. Read it through at the beginning and make sure you are clear about how many questions you need to answer and how many marks will be awarded for each question.

2) **Manage your time**. Allot a certain amount of time to each question or section and stick to it. When the time is up, move on to the next part even if you haven't finished – you have more of a chance of a high mark if you provide unfinished answers for four out of four questions; two out of four questions, no matter how well answered, may well only give you a mark out of a maximum of 50%.

3) **Answer the question**. Read and highlight key terms, and quickly plan an answer which addresses the question. Then stick to it.

4) **Make your writing legible**. You cannot be given credit for something if the marker cannot read it.

Practical and clinical assessments

A very important part of your nursing studies will be **practice assessments**, and **clinical skills assessments**.

Practice assessments test your achievement of practice competencies **in vivo**, in other words, in real-life clinical settings, for example:

- the student is able to introduce themselves to patients and relatives in a courteous and professional manner;
- the student is able to take measures of patients' vital signs safely, record them accurately, and alert appropriate colleagues if there are any irregularities.

These competencies are usually listed in a practice assessment document (printed or electronic) that you take into practice with you. A **mentor** judges you on these competencies and signs them off one by one when she or he deems you competent in them. Clinical skills assessments test your abilities **in vitro**, in the lab.

You may also be tested in **Objective Structured Clinical Examinations (OSCEs)**, which are a specific and flexible form of clinical skills assessment. OSCEs involve several stations in a circuit, for example:

- station 1: urine testing;
- station 2: taking blood pressure;
- station 3: interviewing a patient.

Each station has its own assessor and the task itself often involves some form of 'simulation', for example, simulated patients (actors or mannequins), or simulated pathological specimens (eg simulated urine).

Feedback on academic work

One of the most important roles that lecturers perform is to give feedback to students on the work they produce. There are two types of feedback: **formative** and **summative** (see Table 6.1).

Formative feedback is advice on how you can improve your work in a current or future task. It can be given for both assessed and non-assessed assignments. Summative feedback is the feedback you receive on an assessed piece of work, often at the end of a module or programme of study, to enable you to understand why a particular mark has been awarded; it tells you how you have met, or failed to meet, the marking criteria attached to the task. It may be combined with formative feedback if appropriate.

These days, feedback on written assignments is often provided on VLEs. Students can access their assignment and view comments posted in the text itself, and in the accompanying critical commentary.

No matter what mark you receive for an assignment, it is very important to know why you did or didn't do well. It is crucial that you access and understand feedback, whether it be provided on your VLE or in conversation with a lecturer. Your response to feedback will help determine your future academic development.

Universities are becoming increasingly aware of the importance of good feedback to students. This has been underlined by the introduction of the National Student Survey (see www. thestudentsurvey.com), a survey of all final-year undergraduates in the UK to assess their opinions of the quality of their degree programmes. You should be aware of what systems your university has in place to enable it to meet the requirements of students. You should also be aware of what constitutes good practice in terms of providing feedback.

Good practice in feedback

Feedback should be:

1) **Transparent**. It should be clear how the mark was arrived at. This may involve highlighting of the descriptors or comments which directly refer to these.

2) **Constructive**. The marker should provide clear, helpful suggestions on how you can improve.

3) **Personalised**. The feedback should be clearly related to your unique piece of work. It should also be geared towards your own personal academic development.

4) **Timely**. Feedback dates should be given in advance. These dates should be made in time to inform any future assignments.

5) **Ongoing**. Feedback is not confined to assessments; you should receive feedback regularly, in class, in clinical practice, and through the VLE.

> (Adapted from University of Manchester School of Nursing, Midwifery & Social Work, 2014)

Your response to feedback

It is important that you do not waste the valuable resource that feedback is. You should always:

1) **Be proactive**. Seek out feedback by reading all your university emails and checking your VLE on a regular basis. If you don't understand the feedback, email your lecturer to make an appointment, or visit them during office hours.

2) **Be reflective**. Read or listen to feedback very carefully and make sure it makes sense to you. Consider feedback with reference to the assessment guidelines and descriptors – did you understand the task and follow instructions? Be honest with yourself about whether or not the mark and the feedback match your own expectations and the effort you put in. What can you learn from the comments? What insights can you gain on your strengths and weaknesses? Is there anything you need to do differently in future assignments?

3) **Be realistic**. If there seems to be rather a lot of negative feedback, it is easy to feel overwhelmed. Try to pull out three things which seem to be particularly important (common areas of concern include: lack of a clear structure; overly descriptive work, lacking in critical analysis; lack of research or understanding; poor grammar/punctuation/sentence structure), or which have also been mentioned in other feedback.

How you respond to feedback will partly determine your academic and professional development. It is hard to hear criticism, but it is crucial not to take it personally: the feedback is about your assignment; it is not about you. The main objective of feedback is to help you, so you need to approach it with this in mind. Before you look at feedback, prepare yourself mentally to look for things to learn rather than things to dwell on negatively. It is largely how you react to constructive criticism which will determine how you develop in your study and work life.

Case studies

- Look at the marks and feedback received by student nurses for their essays, and answer the questions below.

  1) What can each student learn from the comments?

  2) What are the strengths and weaknesses of the essay?

  3) What action should the student take immediately or in the long term?

  4) What should the student do differently in the next assignment?

  5) What three points should the student focus on?

Student 1

Overall mark awarded: 58%

- Interpretation of source material 54%

  You have conveyed a reasonable understanding of the material presented, though there is some irrelevant or peripheral material in your submission.

- Critical ability 58%

  You have made some good critical comments about some of the source material you have looked at but, in some of the material, you missed some of the major shortcomings.

- Research awareness 52%

  You have a reasonable understanding of the research methodologies employed in the source material you used, though there were some misunderstandings and inaccuracies in your interpretation.

- Style and presentation 76%

  A well-written piece, with a logical flow and a high standard of English; presented to a high standard.

- Referencing and use of the literature 55%

  Reasonable range of scholarly reviews and sources consulted; some referencing errors both in-text and in the construction of the final reference list.

- Application to practice 52%

  A reasonable attempt to link theory to practice, though some of the links you made were a little weak.

Student 2

Overall mark awarded: 82%

- Interpretation of source material 84%

  You have thoroughly rejected inappropriate and irrelevant source material and have accurately and confidently conveyed understanding of the material you have used.

- Critical ability 78%

  You fully understand the source material you have used, making detailed and appropriate critical comments; strong arguments have been made throughout the submission, occasionally you have missed a key shortcoming in one of the sources consulted.

- Research awareness 82%

  You have a thorough understanding of the research methodologies employed in the source material you consulted, accurately describing, interpreting and evaluating those methodologies. You were very slightly confused over some statistical elements but these are complex areas that many graduates, that many students, get confused about.

- Style and presentation 88%

  Extremely well-written piece, with a logical flow; presented to a very high standard with few typographical, grammatical or spelling errors.

- Referencing and use of the literature 75%

  Extensive range of scholarly reviews and sources consulted; there were a few minor referencing errors.

- Application to practice 82%

  Clear links between the material you cited and clinical practice; clear evidence of evidence-based practice; some additional practice examples would have enhanced the submission.

Summary

This chapter has examined the aims of assessment and detailed the assessment procedure in higher education. It has provided advice on how to approach assessment tasks, manage stress and anxiety, and achieve success. Finally, it has discussed the issue of feedback and the crucial role it plays in your academic development.

Reference

University of Manchester School of Nursing, Midwifery & Social Work (2014) *Understanding Assessment and Feedback: A Student Guide* [internal publication]. Manchester: University of Manchester.

LIBRARY, UNIVERSITY OF CHESTER

Appendix:
The language of higher education

Assessment	Tasks and processes used to determine the level of your knowledge and skills
Blended learning	Learning which combines traditional classroom study and web-based learning
Collaborative learning	Working collectively and co-operatively with other students
Continuing professional development (CPD)	The learning activities that professionals engage in order to develop their knowledge and skills throughout their career
Credit	Credits are awarded to students in recognition of the completion of a unit. (The number of credits allocated is based on the notional hours of learning needed to complete the unit successfully.)
Critical thinking	The process of analysing and evaluating information and ideas, and demonstrating how this process has informed your own understanding, ideas and opinions
Degree	A qualification awarded on successful completion of a course in HE
Diploma	A qualification awarded by a university, which is at a lower level than a degree
Directed study	Independent study under the guidance of a staff member
Distance learning	Learning where the student mainly studies from home via correspondence, using web-based resources – perhaps occasionally attending university workshops etc
Facilitator	A teacher who helps facilitate your learning rather than teaching you directly, enabling a two-way process between student and teacher
Formative	Describes work that you are asked to do which is developmental rather than formally assessed (compare with summative)
Further education (FE)	Education beyond secondary school but at pre-degree level
Higher education (HE)	Education at university level, including certificates, diplomas and degrees
Independent learning	Learning which is directed by the student
Learning outcomes	What you will be able to do or understand by the end of the course
Lecture	An educational talk to a (usually large) group of students
Lecturer	A member of staff who has significant teaching, and often significant research, commitments
Lifelong learning	Refers to a view that learning occurs throughout life and that there are opportunities for learning at all ages and not just when you are a child or young adult (a view that is supported by the government and most educators)

Module	One of the units that make up a complete course at university
Office hours	The times when your lecturer is officially available, usually to discuss problems or queries, or to provide individual guidance
Portfolio	A personal record (normally written) of your learning experiences (increasingly seen as a valuable tool to aid student learning; the best portfolios include reflective aspects)
Postgraduate	Study undertaken once you have a Bachelor's degree (two further degrees are available at postgraduate level – the Master's degree and the Doctorate – though sub-degree awards such as Postgraduate Certificates (PGCert) and Postgraduate Diploma (PGDip) may also be available).
Problem-based learning (PBL)	PBL is a form of 'enquiry based learning' (EBL), an umbrella term for learning in groups where enquiry (asking questions and investigating) is central to the process. It is an innovative type of learning designed to help students develop their thought processes (and, indeed, their clinical practices). PBL involves finding solutions to real-world problems by working co-operatively with other students. In PBL, teachers act as facilitators rather than teachers.
Professor	A senior grade of the teaching/research staff, normally given for exceptional contribution to a particular field of study
Programme of study	The overall course of study you are undertaking, such as a diploma or degree
Reflection	Thinking about and questioning your own experiences, thoughts and behaviour in order to enhance personal, academic and professional development
Seminar	A formally timetabled, small group discussion normally facilitated by a teacher or lecturer
Student autonomy	The ability to take charge of your own learning and development
Summative	Describes work that you are asked to do which is formally assessed, and must be completed and passed if you are to continue your programme of study (compare with formative)
Syllabus	A description of the content you will cover in the module or course
Tertiary education	Education beyond secondary school, including further and higher education
Tutorial	Tuition given to an individual or small group
Undergraduate	Study undertaken at or below Bachelor's degree level (the Bachelor's-with-Honours degree is the benchmark university award and in the strictest sense of the word, you don't graduate until you have this degree. Bachelor's degrees are sometimes called 'first degrees' to differentiate them from higher degrees that are normally taken as second or third degrees. Don't confuse these with the gradings (1st, 2:1, 2:2 and 3rd) that are given to first degrees.)
Virtual Learning Environment (VLE)	A web-based platform to support course delivery in universities
Vocational qualification	Qualification aimed at developing skills for employment, often including work-based experience

Answer key

Chapter 1

Top tips, Lectures

4)

eg = for example

NB = note

cf = compare and contrast

ie = that is to say

Chapter 3

Academic phrasebank, Task

A5, B4, C3, D1, E7, F6

Chapter 4

Scrutinising research and arguments, Task (page 46)

Premise	Ideas on which subsequent ideas or actions are based
Assumption	Something which is accepted as true without question or proof
Agenda	A reason for doing something which is often not directly declared
Anecdotal	Based on personal experience rather than research
Bias	The action of supporting or opposing someone or something in an unfair way, allowing personal opinion to influence your judgement
Subjective	Based on personal beliefs and feelings, rather than on facts
Unsubstantiated	Not supported by facts

Scrutinising research and arguments, Task (page 47)

Introduction

Mental health problems in children and young people are a major public health issue. In the UK, as many as one in five children and young people will experience developmental, emotional or behavioural problems and approximately 10% will have a mental disorder that meets diagnostic criteria (Green *et al.* 2005).

> General context: laying ground for research with reference to the literature

As mental health problems in the general population frequently commence in adolescence (Kessler *et al.* 2005), there is a strong case for embedding the skills of recognition and basic management into wider health and education services. Indeed, school-based services for early identification and intervention and for care coordination in primary care are advocated in the USA (Taras 2004) and in many other European countries (Braddick *et al.* 2009).

> General context: laying ground for research with reference to the literature

In the UK, child and adolescent mental health service provision ('CAMHS') exists under the auspices of a four-tier model that reflects increasing levels of specialisation and case complexity. Tier 1 encompasses anyone working in universal children's services (including teachers and school nurses); Tier 2 workers are the unidisciplinary specialists (such as psychologists) working in primary and community-oriented care; Tier 3 services are provided mainly by multidisciplinary teams working in outpatient (sometimes day care) services; Tier 4 provision – which equates largely with hospitalisation – is for the minority with the most complex needs (CAMHS Review, 2008). Primary-oriented care and community-oriented care are thus an inherent part of CAMHS, <u>yet</u> this provision is often <u>overlooked</u>. For many, CAMHS is synonymous with Tiers 3 and 4 or, at the very least, it begins at Tier 2. These higher tier services are often <u>overstretched</u>, with many having long waiting lists (Clarke *et al.* 2003, Etheridge 2004, CAMHS Review 2008). Moreover, in-patient (Tier 4) services are <u>expensive</u>, both for the service provider and for the families receiving the service (Jacobs *et al.* 2004).

> General context: laying ground for research with reference to the literature

> **Problem** introduced with reference to the literature; 'yet' suggests a surprising fact given what has just been said; note the negative language

There have been calls to enhance service provision at the lower tiers (NHS HAS 1995, Audit Commission 1999, CAMHS Review 2008). Schools often feature in these calls: they are, after all, rooted in the community and are a normal part of childhood. Indeed, Appleton (2000) argues that schools are primary care CAMHS provision. <u>However</u>, while schools certainly have the potential to improve children's mental health, there is <u>little clarity</u> over who should take the lead. Those earmarked for the job have tended to be education rather than health professionals – teachers, school counsellors and educational psychologists, for example – and while few would question the need for interdisciplinary collaboration in children's services, <u>it is odd not to see</u> health professionals taking a lead on what is essentially a health issue.

> Specific context, with reference to the literature

> **Problem** introduced; 'however' suggests what has been said previously is not the whole story; note the negative phrasing

Of the health professionals who could take the lead, school nurses are a natural choice. Unlike specialist CAMHS workers, they are part of the normal experience of growing up and are consequently more accessible and less stigmatising. They are a key aspect of universal health services, and surveys and consultations in the UK and elsewhere indicate that they have considerable involvement in identifying and addressing mental health issues (DeBell 2006, Haddad *et al.* 2010), an activity to which they would like to devote more time (Ball 2009).

> Specific context, with reference to the literature

Background

Reviews and guidelines from the UK (NICE 2005, 2008, 2009), other European nations (Stengård & Appelqvist-Schmidlechner 2010), Canada (Zuckerbrot *et al.* 2007) and the USA (Olin & Hoagwood 2002, AACAP, 2009) recommend developing the capacity and quality of school- and primary care-based support for common mental disorders, with school nurses being key to this activity. However, there is relatively little research concerning school nurses and mental health work. Although studies have been conducted in the UK's constituent countries and in Sweden and France, most work in this area has been undertaken in the USA. Puskar and Bernardo (2007), Bullock *et al.* (2002) and DeSocio *et al.* (2006), for example, provide evidence that school nurses can be successfully involved in mental health screening, promotion and early intervention activities.

Introducing a 'gap' in the research

Reviewing the relevant literature

In the UK, Leighton *et al.* (2003) undertook a small survey of school nurses together with a small-scale evaluation of a school nurse training programme in England, while Wilson *et al.* (2008) undertook a larger survey of health visitors and school nurses in Scotland. Both studies found a wide range of mental health concerns in school nurse caseloads including major mental health problems like psychosis, self-harm and eating disorders. Three studies examined regular contact with CAMHS professionals: Richardson and Partridge (2000) evaluated the provision of monthly consultations by CAMHS professionals to school nurse teams; Clarke *et al.* (2003) looked at the provision of psychologist-led monthly supervision and training sessions; and Chipman and Gooch (2003) examined a school-based, school nurse-led clinic for emotional and mental health issues that involved monthly supervision from CAMHS professionals. All three studies reported largely positive findings, as did Leighton *et al.*'s training programme. Moreover, in what is the closest to what might be called a patient outcome study, Stallard *et al.* (2007) explored the potential of using school nurses to facilitate a cognitive-behavioural programme designed to improve children's emotional health, finding statistically significant and sustained improvements in anxiety and self-esteem among the children who took part.

Reviewing and discussing the relevant literature

While school nurses are well placed for primary care level mental health work with young people and while the literature details some efforts to develop, quantify and evaluate this aspect of their role, there are also indications that there may be difficulties engaging school nurses in such work – not necessarily through a lack of willingness but through a lack of confidence or limited relevant training (Leighton *et al.* 2003, DeBell 2006, NISHYP 2006, Wilson *et al.* 2008). Pressures on time and the demands of other important public health issues like sexual health and healthy eating may also be obstacles (Ball 2009). The aim of this study was therefore to explore the views of school nurses regarding mental health problems in young people and their potential for engaging in mental health work with this client group.

Introduces problem with reference to the literature; note negative language

Research aims/objectives

Discussion versus description, Task

1)

Discussion (some key phrases underlined)

Mental health problems in children and young people are a major public health issue. In the UK, as many as one in five children and young people will experience developmental, emotional or behavioural problems and approximately 10% will have a mental disorder that meets diagnostic criteria (Green *et al.* 2005).

As mental health problems in the general population frequently commence in adolescence (Kessler *et al.* 2005), there is a strong case for embedding the skills of recognition and basic management into wider health and education services. Indeed, school-based services for early identification and intervention and for care coordination in primary care are advocated in the USA (Taras 2004) and in many other European countries (Braddick *et al.* 2009).

In the UK, child and adolescent mental health service provision ('CAMHS') exists under the auspices of a four-tier model that reflects increasing levels of specialisation and case complexity. Tier 1 encompasses anyone working in universal children's services (including teachers and school nurses); Tier 2 workers are the unidisciplinary specialists (such as psychologists) working in primary and community-oriented care; Tier 3 services are provided mainly by multidisciplinary teams working in outpatient (sometimes day care) services; Tier 4 provision – which equates largely with hospitalisation – is for the minority with the most complex needs (CAMHS Review, 2008). Primary-oriented care and community-oriented care are thus an inherent part of CAMHS, yet this provision is often overlooked. For many, CAMHS is synonymous with Tiers 3 and 4 or, at the very least, it begins at Tier 2. These higher tier services are often overstretched, with many having long waiting lists (Clarke *et al.* 2003, Etheridge 2004, CAMHS Review 2008). Moreover, in-patient (Tier 4) services are expensive, both for the service provider and for the families receiving the service (Jacobs *et al.* 2004).

There have been calls to enhance service provision at the lower tiers (NHS HAS 1995, Audit Commission 1999, CAMHS Review 2008). Schools often feature in these calls: they are, after all, rooted in the community and are a normal part of childhood. Indeed, Appleton (2000) argues that schools are primary care CAMHS provision. However, while schools certainly have the potential to improve children's mental health, there is little clarity over who should take the lead. Those earmarked for the job have tended to be education rather than health professionals – teachers, school counsellors and educational psychologists, for example – and while few would question the need for interdisciplinary collaboration in children's services, it is odd not to see health professionals taking a lead on what is essentially a health issue.

Of the health professionals who could take the lead, school nurses are a natural choice. Unlike specialist CAMHS workers, they are part of the normal experience of growing up and are consequently more accessible and less stigmatising. They are a key aspect of universal health services, and surveys and consultations in the UK and elsewhere indicate that they have considerable involvement in identifying and addressing mental health issues (DeBell 2006, Haddad et al. 2010), an activity to which they would like to devote more time (Ball 2009).

Demonstrating criticality in your practice, Task

1)

1.3 Avoid making **assumptions** and recognise diversity and individual choice.

6.1 Make sure that any information or advice given is **evidence-based**.

8.4 Work with colleagues to **evaluate** the quality of your work and that of your team.

9.2 Gather and **reflect** on feedback from a variety of sources, using it to improve practice and performance.

13.1 Accurately **assess** signs of normal or worsening physical health in the person receiving care.

19.2 Take account of current **evidence**, knowledge and developments in reducing mistakes and the effect of them.

20.6 Stay **objective** and have clear professional boundaries at all times with people in your care (including those who have been in your care in the past) and their families and carers.

Chapter 5

Identifying key search terms, Task

1) schizophrenia; behavioural interventions; mental illness; mental disorder; psychosis; conditioning; CBT; behaviour therapy; rehabilitation, recovery

2) dependence; independence; older people; aged; later life; seniors; hospital; hospitalisation; community care; carers

Index

Page numbers in **bold** refer to Tables; those in *italics* refer to Figures.